How Can You Possibly be a Muslim Feminist?

by Raheel Raza

This book, *How Can You Possibly be a Muslim Feminist?* by Raheel Raza, is part of the non-fiction book series in the *How Can You Possibly*® Library, which includes books, blogs, podcasts or videos. Regardless of venue, each publication is devoted to answering the question put forth by its title. Each question is treated as real and answered sincerely. There are no rhetorical questions.

For more information on the ***How Can You Possibly***® series, please contact us:

www.howcanyoupossibly.com

email: **possiblypublishing@gmail.com**

Other titles in by **Possibly Publishing**:

How Can You Possibly
be a Mormon and a Democrat?
by Clinton Joe Andersen, Jr.

Their Jihad... NOT My Jihad
by Raheel Raza

The Bully Grudge
Clint Andersen

Forthcoming in the *How Can You Possibly®* series:

How Can You Possibly
be a Gay Mormon?
by Mitch Mayne

How Can You Possibly
Love Thy Bureaucrat as Thyself?
by Clinton Joe Andersen, Jr.

How Can You Possibly
Build a Backyard Hobbit Hole?

How Can You Possibly
Secure the Borders with Open Immigration?

HOW CAN YOU POSSIBLY®

BE A

MUSLIM FEMINIST?

First Edition

by
RAHEEL RAZA

Foreword by
ARUNA PAPP

Afterword by
BARBARA KAY

Possibly Publishing

How Can You Possibly be a Muslim Feminist?
by Raheel Raza
with Aruna Papp
and Barbara Kay

Edited by Clinton Joe Andersen, Jr.

Possibly Publishing
www.possiblypublishing.com
www.howcanyoupossibly.com

ISBN-10: 0-9819437-2-1
ISBN-13: 978-0-9819437-2-5

First Printing of this "First Edition": November 2014
Digital publication date 11/5/2014 8:46 PM

1 3 5 7 9 10 8 6 4 2

Design & Composition: Possibly Publishing
Cover design: Possibly Publishing

I Am Woman
Celebrate Me

From the ashes of Afghanistan
Where you bombed my home
    and trapped me in a tomb of dust
I am the woman who has risen up like the phoenix
Protected by my burka–which you see
    as a symbol of suppression
This tattered cloak–is my only protection
From the mortar and shells
That you gift to my land–as you turn it into a living hell
I shatter the bonds, reach out my hand and
Gather the wounded and weeping women of my nation,
Stepping over the blood of our children
    as I teach them to say "no more"
No more–will we be pawns in the games of political power
No longer will we cower
I'll find ways to alleviate our ignorance
    and build walls within which we can learn

I AM WOMAN–EDUCATE ME

I am the woman from a village in Pakistan
Where they threw acid in my face
  because their honour was at stake
Battered, bullied and bruised–I suffered great pain
But the damage they have done has only fired my resolve
To never let them make MY honour, THEIR gain
I forced the courts to hear my case and took others like me
Caught in the vicious circle of male violence and frenzy
In trying to dehumanize us
My disfigured face has empowered me;
The cries of my sisters have given me
  strength in my own strength
I won't be cowed down by cowardly acts
I have found my path
  and will never return to the fetters of slavery
I ask for no accolades for my bravery

I AM WOMAN–CELEBRATE ME

I am a mother from the Middle East
Step-by-step trying to build bridges of peace
Surrounded by bloody hell
Where every shell
Has the name of an innocent bystander
I am Christian, Muslim and Jew
I bleed the same as you
I am wife, sister, friend and daughter
But our lives are devoid of any laughter
When our children leave home,
We are uncertain
If they will ever return

I AM WOMAN–VALIDATE ME

I am a woman of the street
  where I am forced to sell my body
Part by part
To the highest bidder–like a commodity
To those masters of the flesh trade who don't know
That we are women–we have a heart
And a soul that is torn apart
When we are used and abused like pieces of flotsam
Set afloat on the sea of time with no end in sight
We are a statistic on the pages of her-story
Not for the unequal wages we were paid
Or fighting the laws that are man-made
But–for being the principal victims of AIDS

I AM WOMAN–DON'T HUMILIATE ME

I am the Muslim woman who came to this land
Many moons ago
I couldn't speak the language, I'd never seen snow
I was alone and afraid with nowhere to go
For help, for advice about my woes
They scoffed at my head-scarf, my faith
My accent and the colour of my skin–
I felt forsaken
Yet I weathered all this on my own
I cried but I survived–thankful to be alive
In this land of the free
But are we ever truly free?
Today I am a victim again–after the terror of 9/11
My windows shattered, my mosque desecrated
It's ironical–but I am told this turmoil is created
By the very people who wish to liberate me

I AM WOMAN–LIBERATE ME

*The poem was presented at WOMANVOICE on December 6, 2004 to commemorate the **International Day of Action for Violence Against Women** and the 14 women murdered at the Ecole Polytechnic Institute in Montreal.*

CONTENTS

CONTENT *(CONTINUED)*

Publisher's Preface

Although it is the second book in the *How Can You Possibly*® series, it should be noted that its structure and style do not follow that of the first book in the series *How Can You Possibly be a Mormon and a Democrat?*, which was an exercise in dialectic dialogue[1] to accomplish it's own purposes. This book is not an academic treatment of the topic of Islamic Feminism, though that is very much what you can expect from our upcoming publication *How Can You Possibly be a* **Mormon Feminist?**

But there is no style guide to the *How Can You Possibly*® series. Each book in the series is structured and written according to the demands of the topic at hand, but very much subject to the personal preferences and style of each author.

The book you hold in your hands, *How Can You Possibly be a Muslim Feminist?* by Raheel Raza, is a collection of op-ed pieces, with a structured that reflect these journalistic origins. The chapters are fast, often humorous, bite-sized and they are organized (mostly) in chronological order.

Sincerely,

Clinton Joe Andersen, Jr.
Possibly Publishing

---

[1] Mixed in with authorial schizophrenia and hidden jokes.

1

FOREWORD

by ARUNA PAPP

I am honored by Raheel's invitation to write a foreword for *How can you possibly be a Muslim Feminist?*. I congratulate the publisher for taking on this project. Those of us who know Raheel are aware that it is not always a good thing to tell Raheel "It can't be done." She will not only show you how it can be done, but will also make the doing of it look very easy.

To some people, the term 'Muslim Feminist' may sound paradoxical, but not to Raheel. She lives her faith. She is an activist, an advocate, an educator, a mentor, a daughter, a wife, a mother and a grandmother; and there is nothing inconsistent or contradictory about any of these roles, all of which she embraces wholeheartedly, and which make her the remarkable woman is.

This book offers brief, but substantive glimpses into many of the topics about which Raheel is passionate. As a philanthropist, she lives by a code: when you give, 'do not let your left hand know what your right hand is doing,' and she seldom writes about this part of her life.

I have known Raheel Raza for nearly thirty years. In the early days, hers was one of the few homes in Toronto that was open to Urdu-speaking music lovers with a yearning to hear immortal Urdu poetry. I soon learnt that half of the people in attendance were unknown to Raheel and her husband, having arrived with someone who knew someone who had been invited. I was the designated driver for my father, an Urdu poet in his own right. I looked forward to these events.

Over these past three decades, I have watched Raheel evolve into a fervent advocate for women's rights, and I do not overstate when I say that at times her righteous anger frightens me. There have been times when I have suggested to her that she should "tone it down a little, you never know who might hear you and want to hurt you." Her response is always the same "I will not be shut down. I will speak. It must be done. My religion has been hijacked and I will not stand for it."

I recall that at one event in which we both participated, the organizers asked if they could take photos of us. I responded, "As long as I do not have to stand next to Raheel, I am fine, in case someone takes a pot shot at her and gets me." While I said this jokingly, the concern is always there.

My fears for Raheel derive from episodes in my own past. I am a Christian, raised in Punjab under the same patriarchal conditions that govern the lives of almost all Hindu, Sikh and Muslim girls in South Asia. For decades, because I refused to be silent about misogynistic practices in my community, I have had to deal with threats from South Asian men, and even from my family. My detractors are determined to control and monitor what women like Raheel and me are allowed to say in public. They are resolute that issues such as honour-based violence and killings and other culturally rooted practices such as dowry fraud, honour based violence, child marriages and female genital mutilation are kept hidden. Invoking accusations of racism and stereotyping of immigrant communities, they exploit multiculturalist good will to chill discourse on pervasive violations of girls' and women's Charter rights.

As a front line service provider for almost 30 years to South Asian families in which honour-based violence was a serious problem, I looked for a conduit to bring these issues to public attention. Two years ago, I found what I sought in a writing collaboration with National Post columnist Barbara Kay. Together we produced my life story, Unworthy Creature: a Punjabi daughter's memoir of honour, shame and love. Raheel's latest conduit for publicizing these issues is the remarkably honest and moving film, *Honor Diaries*.

Raheel and I have been, and will continue to be, comrades in Feminism's greatest challenge, made more difficult by western feminists' reluctance to acknowledge the particularity of cultural patriarchism. Thirty years ago there were a handful of us. Today we witness hundreds of women from within the ethnic communities standing up for their human rights and, for many of them, especially in the

Muslim community, Raheel is a role model: a modern Muslim Feminist who bypasses today's corrupted Islam to find inspiration from Muslim women of a kinder, gentler Islam of the past.

Raheel seeks to highlight the deeply rooted teachings of equality in Islam and encourages us to challenge the interpretation of patriarchal power over women. We need more Muslim Feminists like Raheel Raza.

Aruna Papp, MA, ADR, MEd.
Chair, Resource Centre for
Culturally Specific Family Violence

INTRODUCTION

GENDER JIHAD

Many years ago when I first came to Canada, a journalist cynically asked me if there was such a thing as a "Muslim feminist"? I certainly felt empowered by my religion. More than that, I felt particularly empowered as a Muslim woman.

I called the journalist back and reported, in more or less these words:

> I am proud to stand up and say that I am blessed to be a Muslim woman. If being a feminist means burning your bra then it's not for me. However, if being feminist means liberation of the mind and soul, then I am a feminist along with many others in the Muslim world.

This did not quite convince the journalist but it set me on a path a learn more about Muslim women who are involved in the "gender jihad".

This was a pivotal moment for me, in two ways. First, this was when I realized that I wanted to stand up and speak publically about Muslim women. Secondly, I realized that, in order to do so, I needed to better understand myself, to take an honest look at understanding my own spiritual and intellectual journey.

This was important twenty years ago and it is even more important today as we see Muslim women take an important role in the uprisings against dictatorships and tyrants in many parts of the Muslim world.

However, I feel that western media is still a bit be-fuddled about who we are. They tend to judge us more through our outer coverings than what is in our minds and hearts.

I grew up in a culture where women were supposed to be seen and not heard. In fact, my mother would turn in her grave if she knew that I am now invited to 'speak' at events! But I was always a bit of a rebel. I was also relentless in asking "why?". I found many answers in the works of eminent scholars and academics like Dr. Amina Wadud and Margot Badran (among others). Their work fascinated me and I thank them for setting the ground-work in which grass roots women like me found our identity and strength.

I look upon the early women of Islam as my role models Khadija, Fatima, Ayesha and Zainab–all knew Mohammed personally–were not shrinking violets but women who stood up and were counted. It's sad that their histories are buried under an avalanche of misinformation and ignorance. But their deeds are known and their stature cannot be denied. This is something no one can take away from me.

My path has not been without its challenges. I am able to proudly call myself a feminist because I have the support of men in my family–my father, my husband, my two sons and now my grandsons. It is of paramount importance that this movement be supported by a few good men because patriarchal cultures have been the reason many women have not been able to speak out or reclaim their rights. My sons have stood as bodyguards when I am addressing a controversial challenging issue. These men have to also take some flack. My husband is some-times pulled aside and asked by orthodox Muslim men why he gives me so much freedom.

He would smile his calm smile, take them aside and confidentially whisper to them "no worries–she also beats me everyday". After this, they stopped bugging him. If it were not for his sense of humor and quick thinking, I would not be where I am.

The concept of Islamic feminism has many perspectives and since Muslim women are not a monolith, they understand this concept in different ways. My understanding of Islam and feminism has come from a lifetime of actions, reactions and interactions with people of all faiths.

What you will find in these pages is a mere glimpse of my own personal journey. And as a personal journey, my opinions, experiences and conclusions should not be viewed as representing any kind of a general trend.

This book contains interviews with women whom I consider to be the movers and shakers of Islamic feminism. Yet, what you will read is a mere sampling of what is truly out there. These women represent a mere fraction of those whom I have come to know in my lifetime: "a drop in the bucket," as they say. And were I to include every interaction with every Muslim feminist that ever crossed my path, it would fill several volumes. And yet, while my experiences "fill the bucket" so to speak, the story of "gender jihad" is an ocean of happenings when compared to my mere bucket, full and varied as it may be.

The world of Islam is not monolithic. And neither is the world of gender jihad, within Islam or outside it. It is my hope that the experiences and ponderings found within these pages will help the reader get a small but potent glimpse of that world.

PART 1

COMING TO GRIPS WITH INTERPRETATION

Shaking Hands with Sharia

1996

A few weeks ago, I was invited by the University Summit to participate in a panel discussion on why Muslims are misrepresented by Western media. Next to me, was a man, young enough to be my son, who made an excellent hi-tech presentation and at the end when everyone was milling around saying "good work", I held out my hand to congratulate him as well. He pulled his hand back and said solemnly with a straight face, "I don't shake hands with women"! To say I was shocked would be an understatement. Not only did I find his attitude disrespectful, I wanted to challenge him and ask why he was there; whether he was afraid of women or his own sexuality? But I held my tongue because that would mean making a mockery out of Muslims, which is exactly what we were there to discuss. It's not a coincidence that my paper talked about the fact that we create our own propaganda. As I fumed about this incident, someone kindly pointed out that certain restrictive misinterpretations of Islam condemn shaking hands with the opposite sex. I reminded them that people judging actions of Muslims without looking at the intention, have a small view of moral and spiritual issues.

A few days later, I was giving a talk on Islam and Women at a Human Rights event. A youth remarked that maybe my message would be more meaningful and have a better impact if I covered my head! At the risk of being told (which I have!) 'you have amazing eye contact for a Muslim woman', I looked him straight in the eye and said, "were you listening to the message or looking at the highlights in my hair?" It's this kind of monitoring rampant in our faith that makes me wonder about bickering over mundane petty issues that reduce the status of God to a mere policeman and move us away from the beautiful message of love, compassion, justice and truth.

In this particular case, I made the point of telling the young man distinctly that the injunction for modesty is for both men and women. However, since men have always interpreted sharia, they spend more time telling women how to be women, thus losing sight of the actual message. In this process, I gained some valuable insight on the controversial topic of interpretation, which continues to cause confusion amongst Muslims.

A friend sent me an article by Holly Lebowitz Rossi from the Religion News Service called "Scholars say that the Battle for the Soul of Islam Neither Accurate nor Appropriate". In this article, the author quotes Sulayman Nyang, professor of African and Islamic Studies at Howard University in Washington D.C., who says we should be asking who controls the power of interpretation of the Muslim belief system or din in Arabic (pronounced deen) "The battle is for what that din means.... today".

Nyang is obviously referring to the emerging trend in some countries to enforce sharia Law, as we see happening in Pakistan today. Nyang says "there is this contestation over who defines Islam and who can use his or her interpretation of Islam to justify the right of certain people to govern". This point resonates in my conscience as I watch the so called sharia laws being used to specifically target women and suppress their human rights. In some cases women interpret sharia to their own detriment, as in the case of the Muslim woman in Florida who insists on getting her driving license without a photo, and has sued the court for wishing to implement the law. (Despite the fact that thousands of Muslim women in hijab drive with their photos on their licenses.) My interpretation of this case is simple—follow the laws of the land, or choose to live happily in a place like Saudi Arabia where women aren't allowed to drive anyway—

that's their interpretation of the sharia along with other misogynist and harsh injunctions over women.

Amina Wadud, Professor of Islamic studies at the Commonwealth University in Virginia, author of "Qur'an and Woman" is an excellent ambassador for women's rights in Islam. Last month she presented a paper at an International conference on AIDS and HIV held by Prime Minister Mahathir Mohamad of Malaysia, who is one of the more progressive Islamic leaders. But 20 delegates, stormed out after Wadud suggested that some Islamic teachings worsen the spread of the disease. Wadud faces the wrath of the extremist conservatives who accused her of blasphemy when she said "Islam and Muslims exacerbate the spread of AIDS and...a traditional Islamic theological response can never cure AIDS". She explained that Muslim women are bound by Islam to comply with their husband's desire for sex, and can be punished if they do not. After being accused of demonizing Islam, Wadud told reporters that she stood by her comments. "My paper just states opinions that are different from others..." Difference of opinion has been the hallmark of Islamic jurisprudence with five accepted legal school of thought, but the ability to accept a difference of opinion has been erased in present time.

Sharia is a body of rules and regulations based on the Qur'an and Sunnah. To follow the sharia means living a morally responsible life. It's ironical that sharia which means 'the broad path leading to water' (the idea of water being fluid and flexible), has been made inflexible and rigid. It's the road of moral, ethical and just activity that all Muslims can follow wherever they live—many Muslims practice sharia while living under the Canadian charter of rights and freedoms, which is not at odds with sharia as it should be understood and practiced. It does not have to be forced as in Nigeria, Sudan and Pakistan where assertion of sharia is a political act, which reduces women and minorities to second-class citizens.

Al-Ghazzali (d 505/1111) one of the most famous thinkers of his time, held that each Muslim must have enough knowledge of the sharia to put it into practice in his or her own life. Nevertheless, other scholars have warned against too much time implementing sharia since it can blind people to the other dimensions of the religion, which are also essential. Sharia cannot exist without *ijtehad* (working out principles), *ijma* (consensus), *qiyas* (analogy), and most of all–*aql* (reason).

Essentially, the laws of Islam must never be distorted to destroy the morality of Islam. Those who misuse and enforce laws in the name of Islam, destroy the moral fabric of society. President of Pakistan, Pervez Musharraf today warned residents of Pakistan against adopting the Taliban version of Islam in the country which is struggling for economic recovery and progress. "We are being called terrorists, fundamentalists, extremists and intolerant. We have to decide whether we need Talibanization or progressive Islam".

Matchmaker in the South Asian Community
June 1996

We're sitting in a quiet corner of an exclusive restaurant in downtown Toronto. I chose this location so we can remain inconspicuous. The two young people with me shall be called Vijay and Tanya.

Tanya, 19, fiddles with her handbag and tries to look confident. Vijay, 24, twirls his empty water glass, clears his throat for the umpteenth time, trying very hard to be suave. I try to blend into the woodwork. With the three of us, there is no question that I'm the crowd. I am their matchmaker.

This is Vijay's and Tanya's second meeting, and their first meeting alone (if you don't count me). They met earlier at my house when the two families came together because they had indicated an interest in finding a suitable match for their offspring.

I set up that first meeting. The two families had never met; when they did, they liked each other. More importantly, Vijay and Tanya wanted to "get to know each other more."

And so, here we are on this chaperoned rendezvous. I excuse myself to get some fresh air. The young couple looks relieved. I give them about half an hour alone. When I return, there's a little more animation on both faces, some laughter (a good sign). All's well for tonight.

As Tanya discreetly leaves for a minute, Vijay comments, "She's lovely, but I'd like to see more of her." I promise to try.

On the way home, Tanya indicates she likes Vijay. I breathe a sigh of relief.

Now the matter is out of my hands. Both families will follow up. If the match works out, I'll probably get a special invitation to the wedding. If not, we'll try somewhere else.

Nothing Bizarre about It

This, roughly, is the typical progression of an "arranged" marriage. Nothing bizarre about it.

In the South Asian community, the custom thrives because the union of a man and woman is more than a marriage of two people; it is the confluence of two families. Simply put, in our community, family is everything.

And so that's my volunteer job: I'm one of those who help to bring families together. But I do this only with people I know.

Matchmaking is quite the scene in Canada because the social structure of the South Asian community here is not conducive to the automatic matchmaking that occurs in Southeast Asia. There, marriages are the natural outcome of continuous interaction among relatives, friends and acquaintances—plus the discreet help of meddling matchmakers.

I consider myself a bit of a meddler, because I come from a generation of arranged marriages. I got involved in this interesting exercise for two reasons, neither of which involves my bank account.

First, my mother was a compulsive matchmaker and always said, "It's for a good cause."

Second, I realize that South Asian families living in Canada don't have the luxury of built-in matchmaking. For them, it is important to "network" and to also have venues where eligible young women and men can meet and interact within the norms laid out by their community or religion–whichever plays a stronger role in their lives. People who know people who have eligible children are always interested in meeting other such people.

Besides, I have a vested interest: when my two boys come of age, I hope someone will return the favour.

There are some unwritten ground rules involved in matchmaking. If the two parties don't jive for any particular reason, it's acceptable to draw back. Usually there are no hard feelings.

Many westerners confuse arranged marriages of today with forced marriages.

Many Westerners don't understand that. They confuse "arranged" marriages of today with forced marriages, which did occur in the past and may still occur in small segments of Asian societies.

There also used to be "totally arranged" marriages, like that of my sister who didn't see my brother-in-law until the day they got hitched. Thirty years later, she is happily married, but that type of union wouldn't fly with today's young South Asian descendants in Canada.

The "semi-arranged" match is the one most acceptable to young and old. This is when it is set up for young people to meet and get to know each other, the families approve and the match is made.

The first time I arranged a match, it was for my brother-in-law, Ahsan. I was visiting England, he was in Pakistan and I got a message that there was an "eligible" young woman from a very respectable family in London. Would I please visit, show a photo of the prospective groom and check out the family?

I freaked. I didn't know what to do, how to behave, what to wear. But I made contact and was invited for tea.

Dressed in my Sunday best, I arrived at the house and was greeted warmly by the young woman's family. They served me an elaborate tea (this was the fun part) and we talked. I met Shanni (the prospective bride) and was immediately impressed to note that although she knew I was there to "see" her, she wasn't coy. She turned out to be incredibly sweet, well-educated and possessed of a great sense of humor (one of my personal prerequisites).

I knew my brother-in-law well enough to realize they would get along together. I showed her his picture and she said, "He's cute." I figured, "This is easy," and reported back to my mother-in-law that all was well and they could set the wedding date.

What I didn't know then and learned fast is that members of the young woman's family have the right to make their own detailed inquiries about the young man, because they are, in effect, handing their child to a stranger.

(The young man's family may also make inquiries, but only with sensitivity. It is considered very bad form to in any way suggest that a woman is less than a suitable mate. The fear is that word might spread and dim her marital chances should this match not be made.)

In my brother-in-law's case, he was called by Shanni's uncle and grilled to the core. Despite being a smart, personable young banker, he was sweating and wanting to run away by the time he was halfway through the "interview". But the uncle was just performing his duty as guardian of the family.

While all this was happening, I waited it out in London and, finally, upon the uncle's approval, took the marriage proposal. It was accepted. Ahsan and Shanni were encouraged to write and speak frequently to each other on the phone (never mind the phone bills).

Six months later, they were formally engaged. In another six months, they got married. Today they are happily settled in London, with three kids.

Not Always a Success

I don't always meet success in my attempts to match people. There was the time recently when I thought two young people were perfectly suited but, when they met, they couldn't stand each other. Before it became embarrassing to all of us, they said, "Thanks but no thanks." Without a ruffled feather, we all went our way looking for other prospects.

Success of a marriage, any marriage, depends on many factors, the least of them being how the couple met. To South Asians, marriage is a lifelong bond of pride and honour, for the couple and the two families involved. If differences arise, the family will help patch them up.

A factor that may lead to the success of many arranged marriages is the expectation factor. Children are told that parents know best, marriage is forever and love after marriage lasts longer than instant puppy love.

Take the case of Usman, 26, who is a brilliant, good-looking doctor with a bright career ahead of him. A perfect match for any young woman. Usman lives in Toronto, is totally liberated and modern, and yet he agreed to let his parents find him a mate.

His mother spent the past year trying to find a "suitable girl" (as we say in the South Asian vernacular) for Usman, but one didn't come along.

A month ago, Usman went to Pakistan for a short vacation and saw a young woman his aunt had arranged for him to meet. They liked each other instantly, met a few times; the respective families approved of the match. Usman's parents were in Toronto and left everything in the capable hands of the aunt. A week later, Usman got married. He is back now, beaming with happiness and faith that marriage is a great institution.

Even in a culture where family dominates, there are differing views of marriage. Anu, 17, is typical. She says that when she is ready to marry, she will accept a match her parents choose, as long as she meets the young man and gets to know him.

"Even if I meet and like a boy on my own, my family has to be part of the arrangement," Anu says. "I won't do anything without their blessing." That would make her the third generation in her family to accept arranged marriage.

Her grandmother, Pushpa, who is 69, had a totally arranged marriage. Pushpa's daughter, Renu (Anu's mother), now 45, had a semi-arranged marriage.

Anu frowns upon the word arranged. "I'd rather call it an *introduction*," she says.

Her brother Rahul, 19, is not too keen on the family involvement scene. "If I love someone, then it doesn't matter about her family. Of course, I'd like my family to approve, but it's my life and my choice. Arranged marriages are old-fashioned and restricted to the Asian community."

But are they? Not according to my Italian hairdresser, who is in her seventeenth year of a happy, arranged marriage. Not according to my Chinese friend who says arranged marriages are still popular. Nor my Portuguese colleague who wishes there were more matches being arranged. Nor my Greek neighbour who finds arranged marriages a great asset in her community.

Then there is Michelle, mother of three girls, a WASP (white Anglo Saxon protestant) Canadian. "Now that I know how the system works, I'd love for my daughters to have arranged matches," she says.

"So when do I register them with you?"

A Silent Revolution

January 2002

The latest statistics on religion in Canada show that Eastern religions, Buddhism, Hinduism and Islam, are the fastest growing religions in Canada. The number of Muslims has doubled in the last decade. Canada's House of Commons' standing committee on foreign affairs has launched a study on Canada's Relations with the Countries of the Muslim World. Fundamental to enhancing those relations is improving our collective understanding of Islam and its peoples.

Women represent more than 50 percent of that society, so their rights and privileges need to be addressed clearly and articu-

> Stereotypical assumptions about us as women in black shrouds are inaccurate.

lately. Awareness of Muslim women's issues is clearly required. The question is, where will that awareness come from?

There is enormous plurality in the Muslim world and major variations in the traditions of African, Arab, Asian or European Muslims. Muslims come from almost 60 countries and reflect a rich cultural mosaic. Like the differences in our language, food and clothing from one region to another, Muslim women are diverse. Stereotypical assumptions about us as women in black shrouds are as inaccurate as the assumption that all Canadian women are personified by the bikini-clad photos in The Toronto Sun newspaper.

Western press tends to view Muslim women by the way they dress more specifically than who they are as a people. Therefore, they have reduced the Muslim female identity to a piece of cloth–the veil. It is rare to have a conversation about Muslim women without using the four letter word, "veil".

Modern, successful Muslim women are routinely excluded from mainstream media. It's unfortunate the achievements of many Muslim women today are buried under an avalanche of misinformation by media. Fatima Mernissi, a Moroccan sociologist, activist and author of many books regarding women in Islam, was born in 1940 in Egypt, the same time feminism emerged in her country. The two have continued to exist side by side. In the 1930's, Huda al Sharawi was a radical feminist, even by today's standards. But feminism, like all other movements in Islam, has its boundaries. Since Islam is a way of life, everything we do is ruled by parameters laid down for us in the *Qur'an* and the traditions of the Prophet. So if I were asked if my brand of feminism translates into bra burning, then I would have to say, no.

Inspirational, ground-breaking Muslim women can be found closer to home. British author Virginia Woolf wrote, "as a woman I have no country–as a woman my country is the whole world." This stands true of the Muslim women who left their homes in South Asia and the Middle East, and came as pioneers to Canada, a foreign and cold land, in the early 1900's. They came to support their families, many of them with no language abilities and some who had never seen snow. But they went far north and weathered more than the winter. When the men failed to build a mosque, it was a small group of women from these early settlers that petitioned for the first mosque to be created in Edmonton. They went door to door on Jasper Avenue, convincing people to join in their campaign and in 1938, the first mosque in Canada, the al Rashid mosque, was named. Since September 11, Muslims and especially Muslim women have been under a microscope. Front and centre have been Afghan women. Western feminists want to liberate rural Afghan woman by removing the *burka* (the black, head-to-toe outer covering), which to the feminists has become a symbol of repression. However, the Western feminists are totally unaware that thousands of Afghan women were very modernized, liberal and educated at Kabul University, which was an educational icon, until the time that the Taliban ruled out education from people's lives and plunged them back into the dark ages. For rural Afghan women, the burka was never their major focus of concern. Their priorities are more basic, like food, clothing, housing and most significantly, living free from violence. However, recent articles in the Western media suggest the burka is of utmost importance for Afghan women. The media was bewildered when all Afghan women didn't shed their *burkas* and run out on the streets bareheaded, when the Taliban were defeated. Ironically, when asked what was the first thing they would want to do, they said that they would like to go to a mosque to pray.

Dr. Riffat Hassan, a professor of religious studies at the University of Louisville in Kentucky, is a trail blazer in the field of women's rights. She says, "God who speaks through the *Qur'an*, is characterized by justice, and it is stated with the utmost clarity in the *Qur'an* that God can never be guilty of unfairness or tyranny….hence the *Qur'an* as God's word cannot be made the

> Constant exploitation of women in Islamic societies is not religious, but cultural. It stems from the huge chasm between theory and practice.

source of human injustice, and the injustice to which Muslim women have been subjected cannot be regarded as God-derived."

Constant exploitation of women in Islamic societies is not religious, but cultural. It stems from the huge chasm between the faith and our knowledge of the faith—between theory and practice. Abdolkarim Soroush, an Iranian scholar, has explained this phenomenon in his book, Reason, Freedom and Democracy in Islam, in which he explains why the religious knowledge is anti-women and why most Muslims are opposed to the idea of rethinking their ideology. Soroush has been heavily criticized for suggesting a reform in religious knowledge and the re-interpretation of the Qur'anic principles of the equality of men and women. This criticism comes largely from the male elite because it means giving up the systems of male privilege. How many men, Muslim or non-Muslim, would be open to that?

This knowledge, if made available, would bring to light that around 700 A.D., about 100 years after the message of Islam was received, women's rights were set into place under. According to these laws, Muslim women were presented with rights to voting, prenuptial agreements and inheritance. They could have abortions up to the fourth month of pregnancy and birth control was permitted. Muslim women could participate in battle and keep their maiden names. They also had the right to keep their wages. In attaining rights, Muslim women were centuries ahead of Western women. It was only in 1929 that Canadian women were actually declared persons and women in Britain were not allowed by law to keep their earned wages till the twentieth century.

Judith Tucker is author of a book called In the House of the Law, which is a study of Islamic law in seventeenth and eighteenth-century Syria and Palestine. She writes about a period when Muslim legal thinkers gave considerable attention to women's roles in society. Tucker shows how *fatwas*, or legal opinions, greatly influenced these roles. She challenges prevailing views on Islam and gender, revealing Islamic law to have been more fluid and flexible than previously thought.

In her book, Tucker studies court records from Ottoman-Syria and concludes:

1. The shari'a courts were accessible and popular with women.

2. The courts took upon themselves the task of defending women's Islamic rights against the vagaries of custom. For example, they would insist on a woman's right to a share of an inheritance or her right to refuse a marriage proposal against her family's or community's desires.

3. Obtaining a divorce was easy for women who could prove one of the following:

    a) physical abuse

    b) mental abuse

    c) sexual incompatibility

    d) the mistreatment of her family

    e) abandonment for a year's time

This same shari'a is now misapplied and misinterpreted to crack down harshly on women's rights, keeping male dominance alive and well. Ironically, discrimination and victimization of women also increased with British colonization of many parts of the current Islamic world. For example, Western institutions would not allow women to open bank accounts without a male's counter signature. Women's assets were frozen and they felt the deprivation of their rights. Social, political and economic reasons also added to the problem, but the Muslim religion became the excuse that men used to legitimize their crimes. What is truly at fault is a misguided, narrow interpretation of Islam designed to serve a rigid patriarchal system.

Professor Amina Wadud, assistant professor at the Department of Philosophy and Religious Studies at Virginia Commonwealth University, has taught at Harvard University and is the author of a controversial book entitled, *Qur'an and Woman*. The daughter of a Baptist preacher, Professor Wadud is an African American convert to Islam and explains that as a Western woman, she would never have accepted a faith that is unfair to women.

Qur'an and Woman is a unique look at the status of women in Islam–a more equal and just status. For 14 centuries, the *Qur'an*, the guiding book for Muslims, was interpreted solely by men. Everything was filtered through male intellect, even women's issues. So, for a long time, men have told Muslim women about being women. This has led to Western misconceptions about the roles and status of women in Islam, and has also set a poor record of human rights abuses in many Muslim countries. Dr. Wadud talks about some Islamic practices that have continuously troubled feminists, outside observers and Muslims: issues relating to polygamy, inheritance, women's rights, unequal witnessing laws and other injunctions that seem to discriminate against women. However, a new and deeper look at the verses in the *Qur'an* pertaining to these injunctions, the context in which they were revealed, the spirit in which they were intended, plus grammar and language variances, do much to clear up these doubts and misunderstandings.

Dr. Wadud also addresses many issues that have emerged in the last two decades that were never imagined or addressed at the time of the revelation of Islam, for example, rape as a weapon in war. Spiritual equality, responsibility and accountability for both men and women are well-developed themes in the *Qur'an*. Through the *Qur'an*, God says: "I shall not lose sight of the labour of any of you who labours in my way, be it man or woman; each of you is equal to the other." Spiritual equality between men and women in the sight of God is not limited to purely religious issues, but is the basis for equality in all temporal aspects of human endeavor. As human souls, both male and female are absolutely equal in their relationship with the Creator and as Muslims, both male and female need to cultivate the same virtues and perform the same Islamic rites.

The Islamic Sufis loved to tell stories about female saints and spiritual women, so much of the Islamic history of female spirituality is told in folklore. There is a touching legend of Lalla Mimunah in the Maghreb. She was a poor black slave who asked the captain of a boat to teach her the ritual prayer, but she could not remember the formula correctly. To learn it once more, she ran behind the departing boat, walking on the water. Her only prayer was: "Mimunah knows God and God knows Mimunah." She became a saint greatly venerated in North Africa.

Later in history, the feminine gender was used in many mystical odes as symbols of divine beauty and perfection. However, these stories and others like them are not easily found in the history of Islam as it exists today. The concept of gender equality is best exemplified in the Qur'anic rendition of Adam and Eve. The *Qur'an* states that both sexes were deliberate and independent and there is no mention of Eve being created out of Adam's rib.

The Prophet of Islam remained concerned all of his life about the status and treatment of women because at the time of the revelation of the message of Islam, women were buried alive, treated as chattels and at one point, considered to be inhuman without a soul. In his last sermon, the Prophet clearly asked men to treat women with kindness as, due to economic conditions, men were responsible for the wellbeing of their women. The *Qur'an* says, "and they (women) have rights similar to those of men over them...treat them in a just manner."

The Prophet's first wife, Khadijah, was a successful business woman who was 22 years older than the Prophet. It was she who sent a proposal of marriage to him. His second wife, Lady Ayesha, led a war, riding into combat on a camel. It has been narrated that when the Prophet's daughter, Fatema, entered the room, the Prophet stood up in respect. Fatema was a mesmerizing public speaker and her sermons have been recorded. Also noteworthy is Rabia of Basra, the first mystic of Islam.

> The Prophet's first wife was a successful business woman. It was she who sent a marriage proposal to him.

There is a widespread belief that in Islam, the female is hardly ever religiously addressed except through the mediation of a male, and as an addendum to him. In the *Qur'an*, however, it is clearly stated that Umm Musa (mother of Moses) received divine communication. Again, Maryam (Mary, mother of Jesus) is mentioned by name in the *Qur'an* and an entire chapter is named after her.

For those who believe that a woman should not be a leader, the *Qur'an* refutes that notion by telling the story of Bilqis, the queen of Sheba, who was a ruler of an unconfirmed location, somewhere in Yemen. Bilqis is referred to as powerful, strong and possessing a magnificent throne. The story of Bilqis, as it unfolds in the *Qur'an*, reveals characteristics of an adept politician and diplomat, who would be in her element ruling any country today.

In political life, there have been no less than 40 Muslim female heads of state. Fifteen of them were formal sultanas or queens who had the khutba (Friday sermon) pronounced in their names and whose insignia was minted on coins. In 1236, sultana Radiyya came to power in Delhi and 14 years later, Shajarat al-Durr mounted the throne in Cairo. On Radiyya's coins were stamped the following words: Pillar of women, Queen of the times—Sultana Radiyya bint Shams al-din Iltutmish.

In recent times, both Pakistan and Bangladesh have elected Muslim women as their prime ministers.

Gender justice is an important issue facing the Muslim world today. The lives of women have been comprehensively adversely affected by religious interpretations. While the *Qur'an* makes note of physical differences between men and women across time and culture, the division of labour between both sexes has exhibited some variations. Sometimes, what men do in one culture is done by women in another society. Their roles are seen as complementary and not competitive.

In the present time, the critical element Muslim women need is freedom to educate themselves to bring about change. Last year, the United Nations Development Program released the Arab Human Development Report, produced by 25 courageous economists and sociologists who asked leading questions, such as, "Why is it that there is such a huge illiteracy rate among women in the Arab world?"

The conclusion was simple: Because of a deficit of freedom, a deficit of women's empowerment and a deficit of modern education. The current dilemma of Muslim women is best exemplified through the words of Ali Shari'ati, a scholar and outspoken proponent of women's rights:

> Women who endure their traditional mould have no problem, and women who accept their new, imported mould have the problem solved for them. In between these two types of "moulded" women, there are those who can neither tolerate the inherited mould nor can surrender to the imposed new one: what should they do? These women want to choose for themselves, want to make themselves; they need a model; an ideal type. For them the question is how to become.

PART 2

WHEN IT COMES TO BLOWS

Memories are Not Enough

September 1994

The following is a fictional story based on a true incident.

My three-year-old daughter, Preeti, laughs as I chase her in the park. Suddenly she trips and starts crying, so I hug her. She wraps her tiny arms around my neck saying, "Pretty scared." (She always calls herself "Pretty").

As I hold her tight and tell her never to be scared, a vivid image flashes across my mind–the memory of a friend, the "other" Preeti.

I often wonder where and how she is. Maybe, someday, our paths will cross again. I picture her now as I saw her the first time, waiting for the subway at Kipling station in the place I consider my spot. I'm thinking, "She must be new, never seen her before." She climbs onto the same car and sits across from me. Usually, I try and catch a few winks but today I feel myself observing this striking young girl with interest.

She has beautiful, shiny black eyes lined with kohl. Set in a perfectly cut face, framed by auburn hair, she wears no makeup but looks exquisite. I notice she wears a nose ring like me and the palms of her hands are stained red with henna designs. When she moves her hands, her glass and gold bangles tinkle. "A new bride from my part of the world," I think to myself, jaded at the thought of how many years it's been since I was a bride sporting bangles and henna. She sees me looking and flashes a shy smile, probably noting that I have a similar "ethnic" look. I smile back and close my eyes to nap, feeling her eyes on me. But I refuse to be drawn into "idle TTC talk", as I call it. I have too much on my mind. My pregnancy is beginning to show, there's maternity leave to work out, and a decision on when to stop my volunteer work as an interpreter with the Toronto Hospital.

When I open my eyes, she's still looking at me, sort of sad and wistful. I chide myself for being aloof, but my stop arrives, so I ignore my inner voice.

Next day, she manages to find a seat next to me. She has such an engaging smile that I find myself responding so she says, "Hello," and hesitantly asks me if I speak Hindi. When I say yes, it is as though I turned on a light and instantly, I'm her friend.

In the next few days, my subway companion chatters non-stop and I listen. Her name is Preeti, "but almost everyone calls me "Pretty"," she says. She's been in Canada only a month and is learning English as a second language because she wants to work. Preeti informs me that her marriage was arranged through a matchmaker in her village in North India, a great honour for her family. Preeti said "yes" over the phone and after her papers were processed, came over to join her husband and his family. He's a taxi driver, and Preeti lives with him, his two brothers and their mother in Malton. Although I'm aghast that the practice of proxy marriage still exists, I don't say anything because Preeti seems quite happy. She has no friends or relatives in Canada and informs me that she was very lonely until she met me.

It becomes routine—five days a week—that Preeti waits for me at Kipling station. We sit together and chat until I get off at my station downtown to go to work and she continues to her classes in the East end. Preeti is like a curious child with no idea when to stop asking questions, but her innocence makes her invasions into my privacy acceptable. "Does your husband love you? How many children do you want? How much money does he give you?" Sometimes I answer, at other times I stay silent, letting her guess. Mostly I listen, because Preeti reminds me of my youth—fresh and passionate about issues, full of energy, while I'm weighed down by a difficult pregnancy, my full time work and mortgage payments.

In time, I start looking forward to my chats with Preeti on my one-way trip to the city. (My husband picks me up to drive me home.) I find her bright and articulate with a deep interest in everything around her and a passion for learning. Taking my cue from her personal questions, I once asked her how old she is, guessing about 20. She smiles mischievously, "On paper or truly?" and confesses, "I'm 16 but in my passport they've written 18." Seeing my slight frown, she laughs and says, "Oh, you're so proper, Mona—you've become Canadian and forgotten how we live back home. If they wrote my real age, people would have said it's a child marriage." Her spurts of wisdom baffle my mind.

As the months pass, I notice a change in Preeti. She's becoming pale, quiet and withdrawn. Once in a while, I notice burn marks on her arms; she says she burned herself while cooking. One day she says, "I miss my mother," and I suggest she call her. She replies in a low voice, "I can't—they won't let me." It's my first inkling that all is not well in Preeti's domestic life. I ask her if she's happy with her husband. Preeti thinks for a while and says pragmatically, "It's my duty to be happy—they paid a large amount for me." Seeing the shock on my face, she continues lightly, "You know my parents are very poor and we are eight children, so when his family offered to pay for all the expenses and some extra, my family accepted the offer. Mother told me that I have to do what they say, not only because of the money, but it's the honour of our family and if I do something bad, my sisters won't get married."

On the verge of telling her she's wrong, something about the intensity with which she believes this, makes me stop. I understand what she is saying because I'm a product of the same culture and consider myself fortunate to have beaten the system by marrying someone I love and who loves and respects me in return. But I'm apprehensive for Preeti, because I've seen similar cases of young girls being forced into marriages of convenience and mistreated. My volunteer work with the community has made me sensitive to the plight of South Asian women and the activist in me wants to investigate more, but I sense a pride in Preeti that holds me back. I make it a point to advise her of her rights, hoping things will work out for her.

One day as I get on the train, I notice Preeti is sitting in a corner looking out of the window, wearing a scarf wrapped tightly around her head. She doesn't turn to look at me and there's no response to my "Hi Preeti". I take her hand. It is ice cold. I ask if she's all right. Preeti turns slowly and my heart nearly stops to see that she has a black eye and one side of her face is bruised. Seeing my stricken look, she presses my hand so hard that it hurts and mumbles out of the corner of her bruised mouth, "Last night I got up to drink water and fell down." I know she's lying but her eyes are bright with un-shed tears that say, "Don't ask me anymore," so I continue holding her hand and hope that some of my strength will transfer to her.

Preeti isn't on the train the next few days and I'm concerned. I don't have her last name or phone number to call. Recalling her bright laughing eyes when I first saw her, and how the laughter has faded away, bothers me and brings out the maternal instinct in me. Trying to find some solutions for Preeti, I ask the social worker at the hospital to get me some material on domestic violence and names of services where Preeti can turn for help.

A week later Preeti is at the train station again. Her bruises have faded but she still wears a scarf. I throw caution to the wind and give her a big hug. She's sort of listless and gives me a half smile. Suddenly our roles are reversed and I bombard her with questions. At first, she doesn't respond but when I insist, she tells me that she is being abused by her husband and his family.

"He accuses me of attracting other men with my looks and long hair and when I said I don't, he hit me and forcibly chopped off my hair. I cried out to his mother and she also slapped me and said I deserve whatever he doles out to me."

The picture Preeti gives me of her home environment is horrifying, but one I've heard before. Her husband works long hours, doesn't make much money and drowns his frustrations in alcohol. His mother and brothers are emotionally and physically abusive with Preeti and she feels they only brought her over to be an unpaid maid to all of them. Preeti tries very hard to please, desperate to be loved, but her husband is insanely jealous of her looks and is constantly trying to disfigure her face. Her sole outing and escape is the ESL class, which she is allowed to attend only so she can perfect her English, find work and bring home money. I give Preeti the names of the organizations she can call for help and she looks at me as though I'm crazy. "I can't complain to anyone–they'll kill me or worse still, they'll send me back, which will hurt my parents. It's probably all my fault anyway".

"No", I say vehemently to Preeti, "it's not your fault but you have to get help before they hurt you more. I've see cases like yours before and I've studied the pattern. Abusive people don't change. You have to get away, Preeti."

She looks at me sadly and says, "Mona, in your world you can think of getting away. I have no where to go."

"You can come to my house," I blurt out.

Preeti shakes her head. "Mona, thank you. You've been like a friend and sister to me and just talking to you makes me feel better but this is my fate. I hope you don't have a daughter because she'll never be able to do what she wants in her life."

Preeti is not on the train over the next few weeks and I'm scared for her. A few more weeks go by and everyday when I board the train, I say a prayer for Preeti. I'm doing my last month of volunteer work at the hospital before my pregnancy makes me too heavy to do extra work.

One day, the social worker tells me a very sick patient needs an interpreter. I'm staggered to see that the patient is Preeti. Her poor face is battered beyond recognition, tubes running into her body, she's on intravenous. I feel sick and have to sit down. After cajoling the nurse for information, I find that Preeti has internal bleeding and damage plus multiple burn wounds.

Preeti slips in and out of consciousness. I take the day off and sit by her side. At one point, she opens her eyes and sees me–she acknowledges with a slight smile but her eyes are full of tears. Hospital personnel say she refuses to speak to them, which is why they called me, thinking she can't understand English. She was brought in by her brother-in-law who explained that she got dizzy while cooking, burned herself on the stove and fell down.

"Likely story," I fume.

I'm alarmed at Preeti's condition. I gently touch her brow and whisper to her, "It's all right Preeti, I'm here. No one will harm you now". At this point I've made a decision that I'm going to take Preeti away from the horror she faces daily. I don't know how I'm going to do it, but I will. I meet the doctor, social worker and nurses and tell them all I know. They are sympathetic but need a statement from Preeti before any charges can be laid.

My husband is concerned that I'm letting this affect my baby and he wants me to butt out. I can't—I'm her only chance. I tell him that I've offered to bring Preeti home and he accepts that helping Preeti has become my mission in life.

Next day, I'm at the hospital bright and early. Preeti is conscious and I speak to her at length about pressing charges, about women's rights and women's shelters. Preeti listens quietly. When I finish, she takes my hand and says faintly, "I was willing to accept anything. He could hit me and abuse me because he's my husband. I only fought back when his brother came to my room, drunk, one night last week and said that since the family had all pooled money to pay for my trip to Canada, I owed him a good time. I freaked out and yelled for their mother but she chose not to hear me. I screamed and fought, my husband came home and they told him it was my fault. So in the end they all beat me. I can't share this burden with anyone else because it's so degrading. I trust you, Mona. Promise you won't tell anyone."

With a heavy heart I promise, on the condition that she'll come home with me until she can face them again. She accepts in a resigned manner. When I come home that evening, I start having acute cramps and am confined to bed rest for a week. I call Preeti at the hospital everyday and advise her to wait for me, not to leave with her family. "Don't worry about me, I'll survive. You get well, Mona," she says weakly. "You have to be strong for the baby."

As soon as I'm up, I go to the hospital. Preeti is gone. They tell me she insisted that her injuries were due to an accident and she burned herself on the stove, so no one could do anything when her husband came to take her home. I wheedle the address from my nurse friend and take a taxi to the apartment in Malton. The building superintendent tells me the family moved out two days ago—no forwarding address.

Preeti's disappearance causes me great guilt for what I could have done. When my daughter is born, I name her Preeti in honour of my short-lived friendship with a wonderful human being. I plan to teach my daughter how to fight injustice and to achieve whatever she wants in her life.

Wife Abuse Crosses
All Cultures and Ethnicities

August 1994

Once again I am
Battered
Beaten
Bullied
Brutalized
Once again because I am a woman;
Suppressed
Imprisoned
In the walls of my own making.
Once again I hear the words "sorry"
But they are empty
Bereft of feeling
Once again I am left on the edge
Of a precipice
Cold
Angry
Frustrated
Silenced
Once again I am powerless
Like all the other women I know
Black
White
Urban
Rural
Once again I want to cry out, run away
Once again I can't
Because the children are mine

Gori is a petite, soft-spoken and gentle young woman. She has a black eye and bruises over most of her body, the result of repeated beatings by her husband. Counselors have advised her to separate or press charges. She has chosen to stay in her marriage.

"It would be considered shameful for me to leave since there is a social stigma attached to a wife leaving her husband, no matter what the reason," she says.

Mina desperately wanted release from her violent spouse of many years. She tried seeking legal help but her husband and his live-in family threatened excommunication from her family and community.

Mina was kept indoors forcefully until she agreed to overlook the issue. She is still being abused, while those close to her simply look the other way.

Gori and Mina (not their real names) are South Asian and living a daily nightmare of abuse and violence.

Their stories are not unique, for wife abuse crosses all cultural, linguistic and ethnic boundaries. But immigrant women often face added burdens and difficulties imposed by language barriers, social stigma and unfamiliarity with Canadian laws and rights.

> Immigrant women often face added burdens and difficulties imposed by language barriers, social stigma and unfamiliarity with local laws and rights.

Within the South Asian community, as an example, "fewer women are willing to seek professional help or counseling," says Aruna Papp, an independent counselor for Scarborough. The majority of cases go unreported, she adds.

Often abuse victims are unaware and uninformed about where to reach out for help. Many suffer from language challenges. Their agony is compounded by simultaneously dealing with adjustment to a new country, climate and culture.

South Asians are generally private people and do not like to talk about their domestic problems. The family is their pride and joy and they will go to great extremes to keep the family name from being dishonoured. Sometimes that means trying to sweep domestic problems under the rug and ignoring abuse and violence.

When South Asians, whose former homelands include India, Pakistan, Bangladesh, East Africa, Sri Lanka and the Caribbean, come to Canada, their social and cultural norms are distinctly different from those of the local population. Typically, religion dominates the social code of life. This poses a huge problem: how to differentiate between loyalty to their own faith or culture and loyalty to life within the boundaries of the law in Canada.

For example, in some countries it is not a criminal offence for husbands to beat their wives. And very rarely does a court case arise out of such an act of violence.

"Many South Asians are living in a time warp of 20 years ago," says Afroz Usman of *Awakening Family Counseling and Mediation Services* in Thornhill. "They have physically settled in Canada but have not come to terms with, or accepted, Canadian laws. When there is trouble on the domestic front, they are more willing to let the elders of the family solve the problem rather than seek legal help."

Usman, who has worked with abused women for over a decade and is a board member of the Women in Transition shelter, cites instances where men from South Asia have married South Asian Canadian women as a means of getting immigration into Canada and then dumped them.

"These women do not turn to the law for help, either because they are terrified of reprisals or because they are under threat of dishonour," says Usman.

The perpetrator of violence in the household is not always the partner, lover or spouse, but may be a relative of the partner, says Papp.

"My prime aim is to educate Asian women about the law and their rights in Canada," Usman says. "Once they are convinced they can live within the boundaries of their religion and culture, and still be free, they can move ahead with their lives."

In many cultures, women are generally brought up to think of men in the family as the lords and masters of their lives. They are programmed to accept their lives as decreed by fate and take whatever is doled out to them.

But the scenario is slowly changing. Papp started the Toronto Asian Community Centre in 1981 and since then has set the ball rolling toward building organizations to help the South Asian community.

A victim of domestic abuse herself, Papp works with abused women and trains counselors and caregivers. She has also made a video for counselors on how to deal with spouse abuse.

"The needs of South Asian women are specific to the culture," she says. "Battered women will often refuse refuge in a shelter because it does not cater to their specific ethnic needs, like language, religion and dietary restrictions."

Papp explains that the South Asian diaspora is extremely diverse and that dozens of different languages are spoken in India alone.

"There is a burning need for more shelters aimed specifically at South Asians and catering to their needs," she says, adding there is also a lack of qualified ethnic caregivers in the community.

Leslie Brown, a barrister and lawyer, suggests that a simple awareness of Canadian law will grant women much needed security and protection.

"Cultural, social and religious beliefs are often the biggest barrier to getting justice," says Brown, who works closely with the South Asian community.

He has found that women will generally avoid speaking to a stranger about their domestic problems; others find language an obstacle, while many others simply accept violence as a way of life. On the positive side, women with similar problems and from similar backgrounds are now forming into groups to help each other and train under professionals.

The interaction and knowledge that others, too, are suffering from the dilemma of domestic violence gives the victims, at least, moral support.

Honorless Killings

March 2002

Strangely, the most disturbing image on the screen is not one of violence but an ominous declaration by some Muslim men that killing women who dishonour the faith and the family is a matter of pride. Three hundred people sit horrified, watching *A Matter Of Honor*, an unflinching documentary on the practice of so-called honour killings of girls and young women by close male relatives in Pakistan. These women are killed or burned beyond recognition if they are suspected of immoral activities which could range from being seen with the wrong person, expressing a wish to marry someone they like or going out alone at night.

The camera pans on to Foqqia Bibi, only 16, who has 50 burns on her body. The only sounds she can make are groans of agony as she cries out in torment. Married against her will, her husband's family sprinkled her body with kerosene and set her alight. By the time the documentary was through being filmed, Foqqia Bibi was dead. No arrest was made.

The occasion was a fundraising dinner earlier this month at the Talim ul Islam Centre in Weston, Ontario to raise awareness and money for the International Network for the Rights of Female Victims of Violence in Pakistan.

The dinner, organized by Thornhill educator Ahmed Motiar, was supported by The Canadian Council of Muslim Women, International Development and Refugee Foundation, Muslim Chronicle and York Region Islamic Society. Motiar, 59, is pleased a large number of men attended the dinner. "Violence against women is not just a women's issue," he says. "It involves men, so awareness has to be raised within a larger framework."

The audience is primarily comprised of Muslims from diverse backgrounds but it also includes a few non-Muslims. This problem is not isolated in the Muslim world; it has a menacing international presence and needs to be addressed across the globe.

Events in Turkey, Jordan and Pakistan have come to the attention of Western media recently, so the public perception is that this is a Muslim issue. So-called honour killings are totally and unequivocally against all teachings of Islam. Therefore, we want to erase this misconception and express a universal message of support and solidarity for those working for the cause of violence against women.

The guest speaker, a professor of religious studies and humanities at the University of Louisville and founder of the network, is such a crusader.

> I've read many books on the rights and roles of Muslim women but have never seen any-thing on the rights of Muslim men. Does this mean they have none?

Riffat Hassan begins her address in a light vein. "I've read many books on the rights and roles of Muslim women but have never seen anything on the rights of Muslim men...does this mean they have none?"

Men look sheepish, women applaud. Hassan, who has been accused for blowing the issue of honour killings out of proportion, explains the importance of the history of her campaign: "If a train becomes derailed, you have to go to the start to see the reason why it got derailed and only then can you remedy the damage."

In February, 1999, ABC's Nightline aired A Matter of Honor. One guest commentator was Hassan, the other Asma Jehangir, president of the Pakistan Human Rights Commission. "Following the show, I received a large number of e-mails and faxes from concerned individuals," says Hassan. "Two important sentiments were expressed: a strong sense of outrage at the brutality against women, coupled with a keen desire to take action; and a concern that the documentary should not be interpreted so that Islam condones or justifies honour killings."

The day after the Nightline program, Hassan founded the International Network for the Rights of Female Victims of Violence in Pakistan as a non-profit organization, mandated primarily to create awareness, mobilize a lobby against honour killings and collect funds for building burn units in Pakistan. In less than four weeks, 300 people had joined and expressed their support.

But Hassan also faced resistance and criticism.

"Many Muslims reacted negatively to the documentary, calling it biased and anti-Islam. They said setting up INRFVVP would only fuel the Western media's propaganda against Islam and Muslims," Hassan says. This reaction was repeated in Toronto before Hassan's visit. It fell upon Hassan to diffuse a volatile situation and counter the criticism with her knowledge and expertise in the field.

"To those who are in a state of denial, I wish to say that what is important in this context is that, regardless of the intentions of those who broadcast A Matter of Honor, the fact remains that female victims of violence shown in this film are real human beings, speak in their own voices, whose intense pain and agony we see with our own eyes.

"By denying, ignoring or obscuring the occurrence of these horrible crimes, ranging from having acid thrown in one's face to being set on fire to being physically mutilated to being murdered...one is neither taking the high moral ground or advancing the best interests of Pakistan."

Hassan stresses the importance of addressing the issue of honour killings and taking steps to bring the killers of innocent women to justice. "Most such murders are never reported. When they are, the police rarely prosecute the killers," she claims.

Ominously, Amnesty International recently reported that "the number of honour killings is on the rise as the perception of what constitutes honour widens. There are signs that honour killings will become the next major international women's issue."

Hassan is aware of the fine line that separates cultural practices from those deemed Islamic. For 25 years, this devout Muslim has analyzed the differences between normative Islam and how patriarchal cultures have interpreted it. She clearly differentiates between culture and faith and says honour killings are neither condoned by nor part of Islam.

"Islam is not the reason these women are bring killed," she says. "These killings are not happening because men are following Islam—rather the opposite. True Islam is very protective of women's rights. The *Qur'an* offers no religious or ethical justification for discriminating against women. If we were to construct a society on the true basis of Islam, men and women would be equal in the sight of God."

Hassan has written many papers and books on the subject. She says in order to understand the psyche of those who discriminate against women in Islam, it is necessary to study the religion in detail.

"Women are discriminated and victimized due to social, political and economic causes. But religion becomes the raison d'être and men use Islam to legitimize their crimes. This is the reason this reality has to be dealt with, from within Islam."

It was her personal search to find a niche for herself that led Hassan, a native of Lahore, Pakistan to the study of *Qur'an* and Hadith 25 years ago. Several years after earning a Ph.D. in England in 1968, Hassan moved to United States to teach and research. A single mother, she worked as visiting lecturer and professor at Villanova University, the University of Pennsylvania and Oklahoma State University before being hired by the University of Louisville. In 1991, she was selected by the arts and sciences faculty as "A Woman of Achievement". Hassan has also lectured at Harvard.

In February this year, frustrated by lack of action in Pakistan, Hassan wrote an open letter to the country's military ruler, General Pervez Musharraf, outlining her quest for justice for women.

There are some indications international pressure is working. In March, the government of Pakistan announced its opposition to honour killings and said it would improve medical care for female burn victims.

In addition, the first national Human Rights and Human Dignity conference was recently held in Islamabad. At the opening, General Musharraf condemned honour killings and said such actions have no place in religion or law. Honour killings, he promised, will now be treated as murders and medical facilities will be provided to the victims and their families.

"Despite such hopeful signs, much remains to be done," Hassan says. "Laws have to be put into place, support is needed for building and sustaining an international movement such as was launched for the elimination of female genital mutilation, and for setting up humanitarian assistance for the victims who are mostly poor and illiterate.

"Support is also needed for conducting investigative research so that hard data can be obtained for a systematic analysis of the growing problem."

Murder in the Name of Honour?

August 2009

The suspected lover of a British Muslim woman has acid thrown in his face and is blinded. (British Muslim woman in fear after friend 'loses tongue in acid honour attack' Friday, July 24, 2009); On the same date, in Canada a brother, father and mother are accused of murdering 3 teenagers and their stepmother in Kingston; In Texas two sisters Sarah 17 and Amina 18 are shot and killed by their father Yasser because he was upset by their "western ways"; In New York the founder of Bridge's TV, Muzammil Hassan is arrested for having beheaded his wife, Aasiya Z. Hassan, who had recently filed for divorce.

> They raise the red flag of Islamophobia. This has stifled all debate and discussion about honour killings.

Domestic violence? Drug related murders? Not by a long shot. These cases have two things in common. They were perpetrated by Muslims against Muslims, and their motive in each case is "honour".

Following the recent case in Kingston, Ontario where three sisters and their step mother were killed, there is the usual denial by individuals and organizations about use of the term "honour killings". Usual because these are the same voices that spoke out when

Aqsa Parvez was brutally murdered by her father in Mississauga for not conforming to his set of rules and regulations. Muslim groups called this "a teenage problem" and "domestic violence". In their rush to deny that this was an honour killing, I believe they dishonour the memory of Aqsa Parvez and miss the opportunity to speak out against the rise of violence against other Muslim women which is immoral, unethical, and unjust. It's also totally un-Islamic. As the *Qur'an* says, "taking one life is like killing all of humanity."

However, these people are also ignoring the rise in such cases, because that acceptance would tarnish the community image. So they sweep this problem under the carpet and if there is insistence from outside the Muslim community, they raise the red flag of Islamophobia. This has stifled all debate and discussion about honour killings.

That honour killings are on the rise in the West is well documented in a report in The Middle Eastern Quarterly Spring 2009 issue "Are Honour Killings Simply Domestic Violence?" Author of the report, Phyllis Chesler has studied more than 50 instances of honour killings in North America and suggests that honour killings are distinct from wife battering, child abuse and other forms of domestic violence. Her research has shown that honour killings in North America stem from the same background and for similar reasons as they do in other parts of the world.

Honour killings are mostly perpetuated by males of a family against young women for not conforming to their rules and regulations. For example when girls resist arranged marriages, are considered "too westernized", show independence of thought and action and mingle with the opposite sex, they are ostracized and become targets of a so-called honour cleansing. In some instances these men from strong patriarchal backgrounds believe they are the guardians of the women's virtue and its' their obligation to control their sisters, wives, daughter and sometimes their mothers and force them to "obey the rules". When the women disagree or resist, they may be given a warning, followed by a physical attack of some sort (like acid thrown on their faces) and then they are killed–sometimes in collusion with female family members because morality is considered a collective right, not an individual choice. In some parts of the world, the perpetrators of these murders are seen as heroes and honour killing is not stigmatized. This raises serious questions about the value of a woman's life.

In Canada, where immigrants are welcomed from many parts of the world, they sometimes bring with them their fundamentalist ideologies in the form of excess baggage–cultural and tribal practices that are alien to Canadian democracy.

This is a serious problem and there are ways in which it can be handled. There should be a two pronged approach. One, by the communities to educate their youth and community leaders about the true meaning of respect for women, giving them the equal rights accorded to them under the constitution of Canada.

Secondly, it's imperative that Canadian immigration authorities and policy makers be aware of problems that may strike at the heart of Canadian values of gender equality and freedom of expression. Potential immigrants must be informed of practices that are outside the realm of human rights and the law, plus murderers and their accomplices must be given heavy punishments to set an example that Canada will not tolerate violation of human rights in any way or form.

PART 3

MEET THE FEMINISTS!

Dr. Amina Wadud:
A Voice for Muslim Women

1996

An unusual and exciting conference is taking place from at Metro Hall in Toronto. Titled, From the Islamic Hinterland–critical debates among Canadian Muslims, the conference is organized by a group of vibrant young people who say "this was schemed up by an ad-hoc, risk-taking, culture-crossing, street-fight-of-ideas-loving motley of Muslims from across Canada."

The conference offers interactive workshops on current issues facing Canadian Muslims like marriage, gender equality and faith in a secular age. However, the keynote speaker who demands special attention is Professor Amina Wadud. Wadud, who is currently Assistant Professor, Department of Philosophy and Religious Studies at Virginia Commonwealth University, has taught at Harvard University and is the author of two brilliant books, one of them titled *Qur'an and Woman: Rereading the Sacred Text from a Woman's Perspective*.

Qur'an and Woman is a unique look at the status of women in Islam–a more "equal and just status". "For 14 centuries the Qur'an as the guiding book for Muslims, was interpreted solely by men", explains Wadud, "everything was filtered through male intellect–even women's issues. So, for a long time, men have told Muslim women about being women. This has led to western misconceptions about the roles and status of women in Islam, and also set a poor record of human rights abuse in many Muslim countries".

Of African-American origin and daughter of a Methodist Minister, Wadud was intrigued by Islam in the seventies. "But" she says,

"I could never accept a faith that is unjust to women and that was the popular image of Islam. So in 1972, after much research and study I accepted Islam and made it my mission to research the Qur'an from a woman's perspective. The objective of my research was to make a reading' of the Qur'an that would be meaningful to women living the modern era". Wadud who is an Islamic feminist, imam, and scholar with a progressive, feminist focus on Qur'an exegesis believes that the Qur'an as the word of God could never be unfair to women. She is the first Muslim woman to lead prayers for both men and women, an act that created controversy all over the world.

Wadud was Assistant Professor at the International Islamic University Malaysia in the field of Qur'anic Studies in Malaysia, between 1989 and 1992. Wadud's research specialties include gender and Qur'anic studies. After publishing her first book, she spoke at universities, grass roots level, government and non-government forums at various gatherings throughout the United States, the Middle East, Southeast Asia, Africa and Europe. In 1992 Wadud accepted a position as Professor of Religion and Philosophy at Virginia Commonwealth University, from where she retired as of 2008.

In 2007, Wadud received the Danish Democracy Prize, and in 2008 she gave the keynote address "Islam, Justice, and Gender" at the international conference Understanding Conflicts: Cross-Cultural Perspectives, held at Aarhus University, Denmark. In February 2009, she was a speaker at Musawah–Equality and Justice in the Family conference, where she presented a paper titled "Islam Beyond Patriarchy Through Gender Inclusive Qur'anic Analysis". Wadud was also a speaker at The Regional Conference on Advancing Gender Equality and Women's Empowerment in Muslim Societies, hosted by United Nations Development Fund for Women (UNIFEM) and the International Centre for Islam and Pluralism (ICIP) in Jakarta, Indonesia, in March 2009. She gave a public lecture titled "Muslim Women and Gender Justice: Methods, Motivation and Means" to the Faculty of Arts, Asia Institute, at The University of Melbourne, Australia on 18 February 2010.

Some Islamic practices have continuously troubled feminists, outside observers and Muslims. These are issues relating to Polygamy, inheritance, women's rights, unequal witnessing laws and other injunctions that seem to discriminate against women. Wadud has taken a new and deeper look at the verses in the Qur'an pertaining to these injunctions, the context in which they were revealed, the spirit in which they were intended plus grammar and language variances, and does much to clear up these doubts and misunderstandings. Wadud who is fluent in Arabic takes time out to explain that many Arabic words have more than one meaning so a particular word can be misunderstood unless the context, in which it is being used, is explained in detail. As a result, her interpretations of the same verses have come out in favour of women, not against them.

As just one example, verse 4.1. in the Qur'an is usually translated as "And His sign is that He created you a single soul (nafs) and created from (min) that soul its mate (zawj) and from these two he spread (through the earth) countless men and women". This is traditionally taken to mean that a first perfect male being was created, and then a second inferior female being. The interpretation has also been strengthened by the Christian version of creation, where Adam was created and then Eve was created out of Adam's rib. Wadud points out that the word min can be translated in two ways: to mean either 'from' or to mean 'in the same type or similar vein'. Furthermore the word nafs or soul is grammatically feminine while zawj or mate is masculine. So this verse can't be used literally as a testament to the superiority of the male being. Instead it refers allegorically to the fact that two similar creatures were created, and they are a pair, as everything in the universe except God Himself, has been created in pairs.

One of the reasons Wadud sees acceptance of her variation in the interpretation of certain verses of the Qur'an, is that in the last two decades many issues have come up that were never imagined or addressed at the time of the revelation of Islam e.g. rape as a weapon in war. Wadud cites social and cultural traditions as well as economic circumstances as the cause of distortion and misinterpretation of the Qur'an which has hurt Muslim women a great deal. Wadud's groundbreaking step towards setting the record straight is referred to as "Gender Jihad" (Jihad being a struggle to overcome injustice). Her latest book, "Inside the Gender Jihad: Women's Reform in Islam", was published in 2006. It not only continues her Qur'anic analysis but also provides extensive details about her experiences as a Muslim, wife, mother, sister, scholar, feminist and activist.

However, not everyone in the Muslim world accepts Wadud's findings. "Many Muslim scholars suspect my motives thinking that I want to start a revolution. They see that I'm a convert and associate me with transgressors... but when they read my book an discover that I am firmly rooted in Islam and the Qur'an, and I'm not out to undermine men, they are silenced. Recently I was in South Africa where a mini uprising took place because I gave the Friday Khutba (sermon) at a mosque, which has traditionally been the self appointed role of men—I questioned the critics and asked them to show me where it documents that women can't give a sermon and they had no answer".

Wadud says that while her mission is to continue her work in finding Muslim women their correct status, there are other scholars who are working on implementing these findings in terms of legal reform. As an academic, she stresses the importance of linking Islamic scholarship with other sciences. "I may not see a change in my lifetime muses Wadud, "but I know I've set the ball rolling and our next generation will bear the fruits of gender equality in Islam as it is recorded in the Qur'an."

Khaled Abou El Fadl
for Reforming Women's Rights

November 2002

Khaled Abou El Fadl, often called "defender of the faith," has become one of the most powerful and controversial voices of moderate Islam in North America.

A regular presence in the North American media, the University of California law professor rarely speaks or writes without eliciting a strong reaction. His post-9/11 columns in major American newspapers were thought-provoking and critical of fellow Muslims.

Noted for his scholarly approach to Islam from a moral point of view, El Fadl stresses universal themes of humanity and morality, the notion of beauty as a moral value, and addresses the place of Muslim religious law in everyday life.

The latter is the challenge that poses problems for his adversaries. El Fadl believes Islamic jurisprudence is the heart of the Islamic faith but has been the victim of entrenched authoritarianism. He openly criticizes countries like Sudan and Pakistan, where many are calling for the restoration of Islamic law (shari'a), but where, he says, "assertion of shari'a is a political act which reduces women and minorities to second-class citizens."

Shari'a, according to El Fadl, "is a moral vision larger than any single set of injunctions or prohibitions."

Invited to Toronto recently as the keynote speaker for the twentieth anniversary celebration of the Canadian Council of Muslim women, El Fadl addressed the issue of reformation within Islam, focusing on women.

A world-renowned expert in Islamic law, El Fadl is a distinguished fellow at the UCLA School of Law, where he teaches immigration, human rights and international law. He has an undergraduate degree from Yale, where he was elected "Scholar of the House." El Fadl has a law degree from the University of Pennsylvania and a Ph.D. in Islamic law from Princeton.

"The love of knowledge is no different than love of God and

To hear him talk candidly and knowledgeably about "dishonesty in discourse" within certain Muslim circles today is to appreciate his own courage of conviction and brutal honesty in exposing his less tolerant coreligionists.

necessitates originality of thought," says El Fadl, whose personal library exceeds 40,000 volumes on law, theology, literature, philosophy and history.

To hear him talk candidly and knowledgably about "dishonesty in discourse" within certain Muslim circles today is to appreciate his own courage of conviction and brutal honesty in exposing his less tolerant coreligionists.

"The *Qur'an* is a living text and inspires you to think," El Fadl explains. "It's a living, vibrant and inspirational text that engages in moral teaching by example—it's tolerant and egalitarian in its approach."

So where has the understanding and implementation of the *Qur'an* gone awry? El Fadl expounds: "The creativity and diversity of our faith as expressed in the *Qur'an* has been demonized by powers of despotism who suppress voices of reason..."

He refers to puritan Wahhabism, the strain of Islam that Osama bin Laden practices, in no uncertain terms: "We must take back our religion from the grip of those fascist-like patriarchs."

El Fadl, an intense person who drinks endless cans of Diet Coke, talks passionately about the crucial need to have coherent discourse. "It's imperative to speak clearly, rigorously and truthfully to testify about our contemporary problems, including the status of women."

The tradition of *shahadah* (testimony of faith) has been forgotten in the modern age, he points out. "There is a huge gap in the way we wield our religion and the way we handle life."

Critical of dogma and rigidity in faith, El Fadl's background gives him reason to say this with conviction: "I was once one of those puritan zealots myself."

Born in Kuwait in 1963 and growing up in Egypt, El Fadl was on the edge of becoming an ignorant extremist in his youth, a fate he narrowly escaped when he decided to pursue knowledge instead. He learned about "cultural symbolism and tools of intellectual stupefaction" at an early age. He ran up against "Hadith hurlers" whom he cites as one reason Islamic intellectual thought and discourse have been stifled.

"I'm happiest when my blood is boiling and my mind is racing," confesses El Fadl, who prides himself on asking questions about everything. The challenges he faced only spurred him on the journey to master both traditional and modern learning.

He readily gives credit to his mother for influencing his life and thought as a jurist and modern thinker. "She was my first teacher in Islamic law," he says.

Beginning in middle school and continuing through his undergraduate years, El Fadl studied Islamic law with distinguished scholars in Kuwait and Egypt, accumulating *ijazas* (certificates) that would qualify him as a *shaykh* (a spiritual master and Islamic scholar). During this time he witnessed the influence of Wahhabi doctrines that denounced teaching subjects such as speculative philosophy or mysticism.

"Looking back at our history, there were 135 schools of law in the first century and a half of Islam, and this is what gives Islam so much of its cultural dynamism," he explains. "It was *kalam* (Islamic inquiry) in the field of theological disputes that preserved the Greek works. Today, Wahhabis denounce Kalam as heresy so we are back in the dark ages of Islam."

It is this philosophy of El Fadl's, his persistent exposure of what he calls "the schizophrenia that has seeped into Islam," his denunciation of Wahhabism and self-appointed religious leaders that has led to the challenges and risks he faces today. He has received death threats from Muslim and non-Muslim fanatics alike and police warned him that "unknown and suspicious parties" were staking out his home.

"I have no choice but to speak the truth even at the risk of confrontation because this is not the Islam practiced by our Prophet. When Islam becomes associated with violence, we have to take a stand."

El Fadl has taken this stand with faith and conviction through his books, columns and media appearances. Sometimes called a male feminist, El Fadl has been known to encourage his wife, Grace, to lead him in prayer. His current book, Speaking in God's Name– Islamic Law, Authority and Women (Oneworld Press, Oxford, 2001), reviews the ethical foundations of the Islamic legal system. In it he argues there must be a reformation in Islam with emphasis on women's rights.

"There is a need to rethink the notion of gender," El Fadl says. Islamic jurists talked about women's rights long ago, "but we have been alienated from our religious tradition."

His book is also an exposé of how texts have been changed to suit political needs and how many books on Islamic law by female jurists have never been published.

To say that El Fadl is concerned about the current status of Muslims would be an understatement. He is extremely troubled about the rise of Wahhabi Islam in the U.S., mainly because its followers dismiss knowledge and reason as unimportant. His critics are harsh and stoop to personal attacks.

"It's a lonely road and I feel sad because the worst persecution I've faced is by so-called liberal Muslim organizations. Their leaders feel they might lose control so they fight at a base level," El Fadl says.

Flanked by his wife, a convert to Islam, and his 13-year-old son, Cherif, El Fadl says he finds hope and solace in his students, who have set up and monitor a web site dedicated to him called www.scholarofthehouse.org.

"What choice do I have but to keep fighting for truth and justice till the day I die?" queries El Fadl.

A solemn thought for one so young.

Reem Meshal:
Weapons of Mass Instruction

July 2004

When Reem Meshal addresses her favorite area of expertise, Muslim women, she receives both darts and laurels. Keynote speaker at a recent Forum for Learning event, her topic was *Muslim Women–Myth and Reality, Past, Present and Future*. As Meshal explored questions of the origin and evolution of women's rights in the economic, marital, educational and political realm of Islam, plus the impact of modernity and the controversies it has generated in the tradition from the perspective of cultural relativity versus universal humanism, she saw astonishment on the faces of her audience.

"I see this all the time. Either because people come with preconceived notions about women in Islam or because they have difficulty with the origins, development and evolution of Islamic theological, philosophical and social thought… or understanding that the broad controversies that shape Islamic theology are outlined and linked to developments in the field of philosophy, law and mysticism." For Meshal this wisdom is armour. "Without knowledge it's easy to become disenchanted (especially as a Muslim woman), it's instrumental in helping me find a niche and claim my intellectual and spiritual heritage," she explains.

> As a lecturer at University of Toronto teaching Introduction to Islam for the past three years, Meshal tries to pass on her "intellectual heritage" despite the challenges she faces as a Muslim woman.

As a lecturer at the University of Toronto teaching Introduction to Islam for the past three years, Meshal tries to pass on that "intellectual heritage" despite the challenges she faces as a Muslim woman. "I get different reactions," laughs Meshal, 34, who has an eclectic group of students, some older than she is. "The non-Muslim students look relieved that I'm "normal" and there are mixed reactions from the Muslim students. Some expect a man or at least a middle aged woman covered in traditional garb!" She recalls how some male Muslim students gasped audibly when she first walked into class.

This doesn't faze her because teaching is a passion and she is well respected for her knowledge. "Some students take this course expecting an easy "A" because they're Muslim, and think they know it all. That's the first hurdle they have to overcome–that I'm not going to give instruction on how to practice their faith, but to teach them about art and architecture, law and philosophy, education and history. So while they're surprised, once they settle in and begin to learn, they're insatiable." One of her Muslim students said "I love this class because we can't ask these questions at home."

Born in Cairo to parents who she says "were culturally conservative but religiously liberal," Meshal was always interested in acquiring knowledge. She studied in a Saudi Islamic School till she was 16 and learned at an early age that "it was mechanical education and there was no depth so I had to expand my horizon." She joined the American University at Cairo where she pursued Political Science and International Development. At 18, Meshal came with her family to settle in Halifax, where she completed her bachelor degree from Dalhousie University. "These disciplines still didn't satisfy me because I had an avid interest in the Middle East, so I thought that a study of Islamic history will certainly give me a good grounding," she recalls.

In 1997 Meshal completed her masters degree in Islamic Studies from McGill University, which she says "was an eye opener and extremely important for me to understand both my faith and the Middle East in modern times." Soon after her M.A., Meshal got a teaching position at the Department of Religious Studies at McGill, lecturing on two courses: Women in Judaism and Islam and Introduction to Western Religious Traditions: Judaism, Christianity and Islam.

Meshal has also undertaken unusual research projects. "As a research assistant to Professor Nahla Abdo at Carleton University, I was commissioned to research the issue of monetary compensation for women who were victims of war crimes in the twentieth century under international law and United Nations conventions. The research was meant to bolster the claims of Palestinian refugee women seeking compensation for confiscation of their lands in 1948 as part of a UN initiative". Obviously, with work like this and her upcoming project titled Veiled and Unveiled: Canadian Identities in Construct, Meshal remains continuously in the eye of the storm.

What are some controversies she faces? "Homosexuality is always a hot button. One student last year said "they [homosexuals] should be shot as they were in the past." So I tell them that the majority of jurists from the three Sunni schools of law (Shaafi, Hannafi and Maliki) ignored homosexuality, refused to legislate on it or make it business of the state. It's sad to see some youth are confused and don't always accept facts. They'll argue with me, "but Islam says…," and I inform them that Islam is not a monolith so I ask who said it? Where is it recorded? Which school of thought? And they're lost–because they've been ingrained in one school of thought at home and never taught to question or read."

Meshal understands where her students come from and helps them to see the light. "I tell my students that in theory there can be five correct answers to every question because there are five legal schools in Islam.

"In essence," she claims, "I teach my class about *deen* and *daulat*, i.e. state and religion. I present most of Islamic civilization but let the tradition speak for itself so they can form independent, informed opinions."

While teaching the origins of Islam, Meshal talked about the common ties with Judaism and Christianity and found that many Muslim students had no idea about the similarity of these traditions. "It's a challenge. I see students who come entrenched in stereotypes and prejudice about "the other" and then I see these dislodged as the class progresses…so it's a feeling of achievement."

Meshal believes that religious education on its own places people in a solitary tower, so the ideal is to combine it with secular education. "Take the misconception about Madrassahs," she claims with enthusiasm. "Few of my students know that the concept of the Western University, the idea of an educational institution like a campus, is based on the Madrassah model in Islam. I try to empower them to pursue knowledge as a tradition of their heritage. I tell them that by the seventh century, Muslims had founded the house of wisdom in Baghdad. It was the center of intellectual thought and a cumulative tradition of the Muslim world".

Meshal sets her own role model. She is currently completing her Ph.D. on the interplay between custom and formal Islamic Law and continues to work on women's issues.

Dr. Azizah al-Habri
Justice is Gender Equality

November 2004

Neither the sun shall overtake the moon, nor night
overtake the day–this is universal justice
The Qur'an

Adept at balancing her life as an American Muslim, Dr. Azizah al-Hibri is a woman who is equally comfortable in both skins. As a Muslim lawyer, it took perseverance, reflection and courage for her to find a niche in secular America. In a 1996 article she wrote in The Technical Law review, titled On Being a Muslim Corporate Lawyer, she said, "I respect both religion and business" and talks at length about how her Muslim values complement her work ethics and vice-versa.

Al-Hibri is professor at the T.C. Williams School of Law, University of Richmond. She is also founding editor of Hypatia, a journal of feminist philosophy. She is founder and president of KARAMAH: Muslim Women Lawyers for Human Rights. A Fulbright scholar, al-Hibri has written extensively on issues of Islam and democracy, Muslim women's rights and human rights in Islam. Most recently, she guest-edited a special volume on Islam by The Journal of Law and Religion.

In Canada as a guest of the Canadian Council of Muslim Women, al-Hibri addressed a variety of topics with emphasis on women. In her keynote address she touched on the current dilemma of persecution of Muslims and their civil liberties. "The Prophet of Islam said that one day Muslims will feel like they are holding a burning ember in their hands. This is what's happening to Muslims in the USA and it's only a preview of what might happen in Canada," said al-Hibri. "Our observation at KARAMAH is that Muslim women have been victimized in the USA; 9/11 affected Muslim family life as a whole, but many Muslim women were hit hard, and they are reluctant to talk about their experiences [due to fear]."

Speaking frankly about Muslim leadership in the U.S., al-Hibri said, "Muslim leaders have been naïve...they were caught unprepared and responded with a knee-jerk reaction which is inappropriate. They missed the importance of engaging in civil society...of building bridges and doing grass roots work."

She continued, "Many Muslims feel threatened by the west because they don't integrate or develop alliances with civil society and organizations."

Al-Hibri suggested one solution is for Muslims to engage in dialogue and debate. "Roll up your sleeves and get involved in the political arena, so you will have a say in the decision-making process." She also asked Muslims to send their second kid to law school. Why the second child? "I know the first one will always be a doctor or engineer," she laughed, "but seriously, it's very important for Muslims to become lawyers and Supreme Court judges."

Remarking on the general condition of Muslims, al-Hibri noted, "There is a rise of kingdoms and fall of democracies in the Muslim world. We have allowed rule of law to be replaced by rule of the kingdom." Al-Hibri has traveled extensively throughout the Muslim world in support of Muslim women's rights and acted as a consultant to the Supreme Council for Family Affairs in Qatar in the development of that country's personal status code. She visited thirteen Muslim countries and discussed with their religious, political and legal scholars, as well as women leaders, issues of importance to Muslim women. She suggested, "We need to ignore interpretations that are totally illogical and patriarchal, and offer solutions based in the *Qur'an* that are feminist in nature."

> We need to ignore interpretations that are totally illogical and patriarchal, and offer solutions based in the Qur'an that are feminist in nature.

On being questioned about Islamic law, al-Hibri said, "U.S. law allows arbitration process which is binding. Some communities in the U.S. that have tried to establish shari'a courts to resolve conflicts, find there are usually two hurdles: lack of expertise and the pervasiveness of patriarchal cultural views among those with some expertise. These cultural views tend to influence their reading of the problem before them and their understanding of a proper solution."

Al-Hibri explained how she has tried to overcome this concern. "In cases of domestic disputes or divorce, the community needs to produce an expert witness (because the judge is not going to send his clerk to study *fiqh* [Islamic law]). We feel the "expert witness" must have women's interest at heart. Our organization (Karamah) provides this service." Al-Hibri is also working on a book on the Islamic marriage contract to provide a scholarly treatise for professionals in the legal field in the U.S. to consult. She said, "There is no adequate reference at this time. This book should help Muslim men and women understand their marital rights better."

Talking about KARAMAH, al-Hibri said, "This organization is dedicated to the empowerment of women through education, research and advocacy. A key goal of KARAMAH is the mentoring and training of the next generation of Muslim women leaders because Muslim women need to take charge of their lives and responsibility for the religion. Western courts are not responsible for getting the correct information!" During the summer of 2003, KARAMAH launched a uniquely designed Islamic studies course, with special emphasis on shari'a. The course was created to help prepare Muslim women leaders address community problems and issues relating to women from an Islamic legal perspective. KARAMAH recognizes these leaders have a duty to formulate appropriate responses to the challenges Muslim women around the country confront in their own communities.

The four-week intensive course provided an introduction to four key areas: the *Qur'an*, the Hadith (reported statements of the Prophet Muhammad), the Sharia'h (the life of the Prophet Mohammed), and major Islamic scholarly writings. The course also included the laws, rights and obligations relating to marriage, divorce, sexual relations, domestic violence, inheritance, dispute mediation and the laws of war. The class consisted of 10 women from various professional and educational backgrounds.

Regarding women's role in society, al-Hibri pointed out, "Islamic law gives women liberty and latitude. It's no longer a matter of choice; male leaders have been dissipated. It's imperative for Muslim women to rise to the front lines and not repeat the same mistakes. Our leadership is to unite and not divide the community. The best leadership is based on conflict resolution and mediation; otherwise there will be no leaders in the next generation."

Clarifying that leadership is not about women's liberation or feminist trends but a need of the day, al-Hibri advised the community. "Put your egos, insecurities and personal problems aside and find those who have leadership qualities and send them for training," she said earnestly. "Fundamental notion in the *Qur'an* is that of justice, and justice is gender equality. We need to examine Islamic jurisprudence and distinguish between cultural and religious practices."

Al-Hibri is also a member of the Advisory Board of the Pluralism Project (Harvard University) and Religion and Ethics NewsWeekly (PBS). She has served on the Interfaith Alliance Foundation Board of Directors and has been a member of the Virginia State Advisory Committee to the United Sates Commission on Civil Rights and the Religious Task Force for the Prevention of Family Violence.

List of Muslim Feminists

This list is NOT comprehensive, of course. This is merely a personal list of Muslim feminists whom I, Raheel Raza, know or have met. There are many others too numerous to include.

Margot Badran

A historian and gender studies specialist focusing on the Middle East and Islamic societies, her interests include historical and contemporary feminisms in Muslim majority and minority societies, Muslim women's autobiographies, and social movements, gender, and democratization. A senior fellow at the Prince Alwaleed Bin Talal Center for Muslim Christian Understanding at Georgetown University and senior scholar at the Woodrow Wilson International Center for Scholars in Washington. She has authored

Gender and Islam in Africa: Rights, Sexuality, and Law (2011)

Feminism in Islam: Secular and Religious Convergences (2009)

Feminism Beyond East and West:
New Gender Talk and Practice in Global Islam (2007)

Feminists, Islam, and Nation Gender
and the Making of Modern Egypt (1996)

Amina Wadud

An Islamic feminist, imam, and scholar with a progressive, feminist focus on Qur'an exegesis. Her first book, published in 1999, contributes a gender-inclusive reading to one of the most fundamental disciplines in Islamic thought, Qur'anic exegesis. Her latest book not only continues her Qur'anic analysis but also provides extensive details about her experiences as a Muslim, wife, mother, sister, scholar, and activist. Her works include

Qur'an and Woman:
Rereading the Sacred Text from a Woman's Perspective (1999)

Inside the Gender Jihad: Women's Reform in Islam (2006)

Aminah McCloud

A professor of Islamic Studies in the Department of Religious Studies at DePaul University and the Director of the Islamic World Studies Program. She is the author of over twenty articles on topics ranging from Islamic Law to Muslim women. She has authored the following:

African American Islam

Questions of Faith

Transnational Muslims in American Society

Silks: The Textures of American Muslim Women's Lives

Owning Islam: African American Islam in 21st Century (current project)

Riffat Hassan

One of the pioneers of feminist theology in the context of the Islamic tradition–an area in which she has been engaged since 1974. In February 1999, she founded The International Network for the Rights of Female Victims of Violence in Pakistan (INRFVVP), a non-profit organization with a worldwide membership, which has played a noteworthy role in highlighting the issue of violence against girls and women, particularly with reference to "crimes of honor".

Asma Barlas

An academic educated in Pakistan and the United States. She is the Director of the Center for the Study of Culture, Race, and Ethnicity of the department of politics at Ithaca College, New York. Her specialties include comparative and international politics, Islam and Qur'anic hermeneutics, and women and gender. Barlas was named to the prestigious Spinoza Chair at the University of Amsterdam in the Netherlands for "her prominent contributions to discussions about women and Islam".

Laleh Bakhtiar

A Lecturer on Islam at the Lutheran Theological Seminary connected to the University of Chicago and translator of *The Sublime Qur'an*. She has translated 25 books and written 20 on Islam and Sufism. Dr. Bakhtiar believes "in the universality of all faiths, that God is one and speaks to us in all languages." Dr. Bakhtiar cites that the word *kafir* should be translated as "ungrateful" rather than its more traditional translation as the word "infidel".

Fatima Mernissi

A Moroccan sociologist, activist and author of many books regarding women in Islam. As an Islamic feminist, Mernissi is largely concerned with Islam and women's roles in it, analyzing the historical development of Islamic thought and its modern manifestation. Through a detailed investigation of the nature of the succession to Muhammad, she casts doubt on the validity of some of the *hadith* (sayings and traditions attributed to him), and therefore the subordination of women that she sees in Islam, but not necessarily in the *Qur'an*.

Huda Shaarawi

She has become a legendary figure in the Middle East and as an Egyptian activist. In the early 1920s, she was a leader in Egypt's fight for political independence. Turning her attention toward feminism, Shaarawi led the struggle for women's rights in the Middle East, focusing on education, voting rights, and marriage laws. Her act of defiance in removing her veil at the Cairo train station in 1923 marked the first time an Egyptian woman shunned tradition so visibly. From this moment on, increasing numbers of Egyptian women refused the role of silent wife behind the seclusion of the veil.

Reem Meshal

Dr. Meshal joined the LSU faculty in 2005 as an Assistant Professor of Islamic Studies at LSU. In addition to courses in Islamic Studies, she regularly offers the survey of Judaism, Christianity, and Islam and a course in fundamentalisms and religious nationalism. Her current research project is "The Informal Path: Sijils and Functionaries of Custom in Ottoman Cairo."

Leila Ahmed

She came to the Divinity School in 1999 as the first professor of women's studies in religion and was appointed to the Victor S. Thomas chair in 2003. Prior to her appointment at HDS, she was professor of women's studies and Near Eastern studies at the University of Massachusetts-Amherst. While at the University of Massachusetts, she was director of the women's studies program from 1992 to 1995 and director of the Near Eastern studies program from 1991 to 1992. Her latest book has been widely acclaimed as well as many articles, among them "Arab Culture and Writing Women's Bodies" and "Between Two Worlds: The Formation of a Turn of the Century Egyptian Feminist." Her current research and writing centers on Islam in America and issues of women and gender. She has written he following books:

A Border Passage

Women and Gender in Islam: The Historical Roots of a Modern Debate

Edward William Lane: A Study of His Life and Work and
   of British Ideas of the Middle East in the Nineteenth Century

Dr. Khaled Abou El Fadl (a man!)

He is one of the world's leading authorities on Islamic law and Islam, and a prominent scholar in the field of human rights. He is the Omar and Azmeralda Alfi Distinguished Professor in Islamic Law at the UCLA School of Law where he teaches International Human Rights, Islamic Jurisprudence, National Security Law, Law and Terrorism, Islam and Human Rights, Political Asylum and Political

Crimes and Legal Systems. He also holds the Chair in Islam and Citizenship at the University of Tilburg, the Netherlands.

Asma Jehangir

She is a leading Pakistani lawyer, advocate of the Supreme Court of Pakistan, President Supreme Court Bar Association of Pakistan and human rights activist, who works both in Pakistan and internationally to prevent the persecution of religious minorities, women, and exploitation of children.

She was the United Nations Special Rapporteur on Freedom of Religion or Belief from 2004 to 2010. Previously, she served as the UN Special Rapporteur on Extrajudicial, Arbitrary and Summary Executions. She is also chairperson of Human Rights Commission of Pakistan.

Mona Eltahawy

An award-winning columnist and an international public speaker on Arab and Muslim issues. She is based in New York. She is a columnist for *Canada's Toronto Star*, Israel's *The Jerusalem Report* and Denmark's *Politiken*. Her opinion pieces have been published frequently in *The Washington Post* and the *International Herald Tribune* and she has appeared as a guest analyst in several media outlets.

Shirin Ebadi

In 2009, with the... assistance (so to speak) of the Iranian government, Ebadi won the distinction of being the first person in history to have her Nobel Peace Prize forcibly seized by state authorities. The Iranian government denies any wrongdoing. In any case, she was the first ever Iranian, and the first Muslim woman to have received the prize, which was awarded to her 2003 for her significant and pioneering efforts for democracy and human rights, especially women's, children's, and refugee rights.

An Iranian lawyer, a former judge and human rights activist, she founded the Defenders of Human Rights Center in Iran. Though her home is in Tehran, she has been in exile in the U.K. since June

2009 due to the increase in persecution of Iranian citizens like herself, who are critical of the current regime.

Zainah Anwar

A widely recognized in Malaysia as the founder of Sisters in Islam (also known as SIS), which, for the past 20 years, insists on justice for women as accorded to them by the *Qur'an*. Anwar and SIS helped defeat a family law amendment, which would have made polygamy and divorce easier for Malaysian men. Through SIS, Anwar has achieved international acclaim in her quest for women's rights in the structure available in the *Qur'an*.

Holding a law degree from Tufts University, Anwar is also a former member of the Human Rights Commission of Malaysia. As the public face of SIS, Anwar gives public speeches on Islam and women's rights, politics, and fundamental liberties on both the Malaysian and international stage. Her book is a standard reference for those studying Malaysia, especially Malaysian Islam. Her works include,

Islamic Revivalism in Malaysia: Dakwah Among the Students

Sheema Kermani

A Pakistani artist, activist and feminist for whom dance is a passion as well as a social cause. She teaches dancing and also acts for the stage and television. She combines this with activism which includes mobile theatre in poor localities of the city. She is Pakistan's leading dancer with a social cause. The performance is, however, not meant to spellbind the audience. It is a celebration as well as an exploration of the meaning of life, personal concerns and social issues.

PART 4

THE FUTURE OF ISLAMIC FEMINISM

Weaving a Web of Peace

July 2003

It wasn't tourism that brought women of various faiths and nationalities to Ottawa last month. It was their passion for building bridges, not of concrete and steel, but bridges of understanding, harmony and peace.

More than 400 converged on Parliament Hill for a conference on Diversity and Islam—Bridging the Gaps, the first initiative of the Canadian branch of Women Engaging in Bridge Building.

WEBB is "an initiative led by women for women the world over, with many bridges to be built–the first one being a bridge between Muslims and non-Muslims," explained the organization's founder and head, Dr. Riffat Hassan, a professor of religious studies at the University of Louisville, Kentucky. "I use the term "engaging" in our title to reflect that our development is active and ongoing."

David Kilgour, secretary of state (Asia Pacific), told the conference

It's appropriate that this first major event by WEBB, as a new international organization, be held in Canada. We consider ourselves bridge builders. This event allows us to see the enormous spiritual, cultural and ethical strength of Islam.

A few weeks before the conference, Statistics Canada reported the number of Muslims in Canada had doubled in the past decade. The idea for WEBB was born in Milan September 2001, at a conference on "Women Leading Global Change". One attendee was a businesswoman from Italy named Louise Kissane who recalled,

> I attended a session by Riffat Hassan, titled, "Encountering the Future," where she talked about the true face of Islam, focusing on the events of September 11 and stressing the need for building bridges. Hers was a message for women of the world and she was an inspiration to all of us. It was a unique moment in history and I knew I had met someone who had the ability to move the world forward.

The next day, a group of enthusiastic women asked Hassan to lead them in a bridge-building exercise. They pledged their support and WEBB was born. It has chapters in Canada, Germany, Italy, France, Britain and the United States.

> Kissane became a key patron of WEBB. She said, I've lived all my adult life in a Latin country and wanted to help women in Italy be independent, stand up and to take pride in themselves.

Laure Capelle, chair of WEBB France, regards WEBB as

> a worldwide family, a web made of women (and like-minded men) willing to promote peace and justice with respect, love and compassion between people all over the world.

Alisha Lehman-Wansing, head of WEBB Germany, wants to realize WEBB's mission to build

> A fraternity (or sisterhood) through a better understanding of each other's culture, religion and beliefs.

Some of WEBB's primary objectives evolved from work in which Hassan is already involved:

- Creating change for women through education and raising awareness

- Educating women about their rights according to their faith, with particular emphasis initially on Muslim women, to prevent honour killings, abuses of power and other crimes committed against women in the name of God

- Establishing a network for women to enable them to improve their economic conditions

- Giving a voice to marginalized women

Nazreen Ali, president of WEBB Canada, explained why the organization kicked off with a conference on Islam:

> Recent global events have focused unprecedented attention on Islam, which is the faith of over 600,000 people in Canada," she said. "The opportunity now exists to foster understanding of Islam, the diversity of the Muslim world and contribution of Muslims to Canada and the world.

Changing the Image of Islam's Begins with Women

December 2003

My cousin visiting from France told me of an interesting incident. While studying for her master's degree in international business at Ecole Nationale Des Ponts et Chaussees in Paris last year, the professor in her organizational management class got an advance profile of all students. On the first day in class, he called her name and asked her to stand up and recite Einstein's theory of relativity. Although she thought it strangely irrelevant to the MBA class, she had studied physics, so she answered the question promptly and correctly. She told me there was absolute silence while the professor's jaw dropped. He blurted out, "But according to your profile, you aren't supposed to know the answer to that question!" The profile outlined Amber as a 25-year-old Pakistani, Muslim girl who, according to his preconceived notion, obviously wasn't supposed to be knowledgeable about science. "Of course," said Amber with glee, "the professor apologized and the class looked at me with new respect after that–especially the guys".

Islam was sent as a system of social justice and to free women from female infanticide, slavery, oppression and bondage.

Muslims, and particularly Muslim women, are fighting the image war at every level. Earlier in March this year, while the world was celebrating International Women's Day, I was battling a series of questions from a journalist about how I could profess to be Muslim and a feminist! To her, this was contradictory and in order to answer her query satisfactorily, I had to go through practically the entire history of Islam and explain a simple fact that many people forget, even when they study Islam: Islam was sent as a system of social justice and to free women from female infanticide, slavery, oppression and bondage. I also explained that, to me, feminism is about equal rights. In theory Islam gives women the basic rights to live, work, marry, vote, have freedom and justice based on the *Qur'an*. How these rights are being practiced today in culturally male-dominated societies is something the entire community must face and address.

Muslims in North America are addressing the issue of negative stereotyping at various levels. A recent Islamic Society of North America conference in Toronto discussed strategies. The able guest speaker talked about "educating the public about the faith". This is an important step in helping the host community understand the issues faced by this fast growing group of Muslims who are now the second largest minority in North America.

I don't know if there was a keynote female speaker at the ISNA conference, but there were no quotes from any women reported. At a time when there are major issues facing Muslim women, they should be invited to be in the forefront of any discussion regarding the community at large.

For centuries, Muslim women have disadvantaged themselves by allowing others to define their rights and responsibilities, and interpret the *Qur'an* through a male-centric cultural lens. But visionary scholars say that every generation of Muslims has the right to interpret the foundational principles of Islam to solve their own problems.

Through a non-Muslim lens, Muslim women are constantly judged by the yardstick of how the Taliban abuse Afghan women or how the Saudis oppress their women and don't allow them to drive. These inhuman actions have no basis in Islam. In actual fact, Islam is nowhere on the mind of these men when they force their patriarchal and oppressive rules on the women. It's not about faith–it's about power. Unfortunately for our image, the Muslim community doesn't always practice what it preaches, so theory remains far removed from the practices, which in some cases, are questionable.

Recently at a lecture in Toronto, well-known Islamic scholar Dr. Sachedina spoke about family rights and mentioned something that came as news even to my somewhat liberated mind. He explained that in a family dispute, the woman's decision overrules the man (provided she is not pursuing an un-Islamic cause). He further explained that any person who dehumanizes another or digresses from justice and humanity is not a person of faith. This lecture, attended by many non-Muslims, was another small step in the direction of removing stereotypes and pre-conceived images.

We still have a long way to go. The Muslim community worldwide needs to practice more of what the faith preaches and harshly criticize those regimes or individuals who stifle human rights and undermine human dignity. It will only be through example, especially in their treatment of women, that Muslims will reach the end of this long journey to liberate our image.

From Ritual to Spiritual

April 2005

Traditionally, Friday congregational prayer is lead by a male Imam and constitutes a two-part sermon given before the prayer. The first part of the sermon is spiritual and the second part is usually political or social.

At the rate poison darts are soaring towards me, one would think I led a chorus line and not an Islamic prayer! Yes indeed, the *fatwas* are flying (I already have one from a Saudi network based in the U.S., thank you!). The Muslim community of the Greater Toronto Area, even those who profess to be liberal, are doing what has become the norm– condemning without considering, labeling

Nowhere in the Qur'an does it specify women can't lead prayer.

without listening and judging without justice.

Let me confess where all this began. About three weeks ago, when Tarek Fatah, founder of the Muslim Canadian Congress asked me if I would lead a mixed gender group in prayer, I said No! I wasn't ready to be part of media frenzy. Tarek and I have agreed to disagree on many points, but we have what I call "a dignity of difference", a respectful exchange of ideas which is a characteristic abysmally lacking in some parts of the Muslim community.

My husband convinced me that it would be a natural progression from giving sermons in churches and praying in synagogues and temples to lead prayer for my own community.

I checked with a professor of religious studies who was an Imam in Toronto. He categorically said that nowhere in the *Qur'an* does it specify women can't lead prayer. Also, during the lifetime of Prophet Mohammad in the seventh century, when he preached his message to a purely male dominated society, he did not speak out for or against women leading prayer. As a matter of fact, the women at that time were businesswomen, theologians, mystics and also participated in war. I'm extremely impressed by these female role models.

The three men in my life (two sons and spouse) encouraged me to take this leap of faith. What more could I ask for? I've always believed that God has created us equal and spirituality is not dependent on gender. However, there are many people who are barred from places of worship; there are women who have stopped going to the mosque because of being stuck near the bathrooms or kitchen due to their gender.

More importantly, all worship in Islam begins with a declaration of intent. My intention was not reactionary, not defiant and definitely not a show of militant feminism. It wasn't about a battle between progressive and conservative; it was about sharing some profound thoughts with my fellow Muslims and also to help other women find a safe space to worship. April 20 was Earth Day. After moving the venue twice (because the so called liberal and culturally progressive centres refused to have a woman lead prayer), a backyard in Toronto's Cabbage Town became the sanctuary. A motley crowd of about 40 people from as far as Oakville and Pickering came to join in this historical Friday prayer, among them an Imam, women in hijab and diverse Muslims from various backgrounds. There was no security guard posted at the door to check I.D., credentials or people's intentions since I don't believe that is our mission in life. I am only responsible for my conscience and answerable only to God. This event was also an attempt to break the domination of a few misguided bigots who try to reduce God to a policeman.

Although physically I led the prayer by standing in front and reading the sermon before the prayer, we were all bound by our united submission to God. I felt we were truly blessed. Why? Because these brave men and women who chose to stand behind me and pray empowered me with a responsibility that made my own prayer more poignant and meaningful. It allowed me to move away from the ritual to the spiritual and actually hear and understand myself better than I ever have. At the end of the prayer, some of the non-Muslim observers had tears in their eyes and were touched to the core. Some participants told me they had not prayed in years and were thrilled to come back into the fold.

As for the critics, let me try and understand where their problem lies. Our message was one of tolerance, peace, spiritual equality, compassion and love of Allah and His Prophet. Obviously, that is not the message coming out of some mosques that base their sermons on negating others. While this is not the ultimate move for reclaiming our place in Islam, it's a fact that our faith is frozen in time. Dialogue and debate, also known as *ijtihad*, an important cornerstone of Islam, have been deemed unnecessary evils and stopped since the sixteenth century. So the hope is that events like this one will open the doors to that much needed discourse and put us on the path to enlightenment together as men and women in faith.

First Sermon

Surah Nissa (the chapter on women) in the *Qur'an* begins with the following verse:

O mankind fear your Guardian Lord who created you from a single person, created out of it his mate and from them scattered like seeds countless men and women–fear Allah through whom you demand your mutual rights and be heedful of the wombs that bore you for Allah ever watches over you.

I believe from my heart and soul that Allah made us equal in creation and wanted all of us to have this equality that is denied to many women today. What we are doing today is not re-inventing our own tradition, rather following in the tradition, the Sunnah of the prophet. And how auspicious is this occasion today, being the birth anniversary of our beloved Prophet who is a mercy for all human-kind.

The *Qur'an* says in surah 2:

Even as we have sent among you a messenger from among you who recites to you our communications and purifies you and teaches you the book and the wis-dom and teaches you that which you did not know.

What many people don't know, for example, is that the early mosque was not only a place for prayer for women, but was a centre for many other activities as well. It functioned as the school, where people learned their religion, and the parliament, where the community discussed new laws and affairs of the state. It was also the courthouse, where judgments were passed, and the community center, where families met their friends and neighbours and held their celebrations. In short, it was the hub and centre of public life for

The greatest jihad for us today, is the jihad to speak the truth. And speaking truthfully, irrespective of the con-sequences, means not condemning anyone or passing judgment on anyone.

the emerging Muslim nation and women were active participants. It's sad that today women have been delegated to the back benches of the mosques and therefore we have to find safe spaces.

I'm often asked where I get the strength of conviction that I'm doing the right thing. I'm inspired by the first woman of Islam, Khadija, also called mother of believers. It is said that her wealth could cover the grounds around the Kaaba, yet she donated her assets to build that small Muslim community which desperately needed her support. I'm motivated by Bibi Fatima who relayed the Prophet's sermons to the larger community. Tradition records that when she entered the room, the Prophet stood up in respect. I draw strength and courage from Bibi Zainab, who shook the court of Yazid with her impassioned *khutba* after the tragedy of Karbala. So we see a woman building an empire through her financial status, a woman stabilizing that empire though her piety and a woman shaking an empire though her passion for truth and justice. There are stories of strong women in the *Qur'an*, stories of Mary, mother of Jesus, Bilquis, the queen of Sheba and mother of Moses to name just a few.

Later, a considerable number of women of the ninth and tenth centuries are mentioned in the Arabic and Persian sources for their extraordinary achievements in mysticism as well as being poets, calligraphers or jurists.

Today, I feel moved that we are gathered here to submit to Allah and pay tribute to His loving Prophet Mohammad. When we celebrate the Prophet's life, we celebrate the women of his family and the other women of Islam. Women who took their direction from him—a man who is a mercy for our hearts in allowing them to open up on truth in all aspects of life, and a mercy for our hearts, making them full of love for all people, and a mercy for our lives as we seek to establish justice in our relations. Prophet Mohammad taught us many things, but one important lesson is that the more you live the greatness of God in you, the more pious and God-loving you become. You would know the meaning of being a human being as well as how much every human being needs Allah and how all human beings are equal before him, with the most pious among them becoming the closest to Allah.

Second Sermon

My friends, the greatest jihad—inner struggle—for us today, is the jihad to speak the truth. And speaking truthfully, irrespective of the consequences, means not condemning anyone or passing judgment on anyone for Allah has clearly said in the *Qur'an*:

Let there be no compulsion in religion: Truth stands out clear from error.

Whoever rejects Shaitan and believes in Allah has grasped the most trustworthy handhold that never breaks. And Allah knows and hears all things. Where we find ourselves short is the ability to speak the truth, even in front of an unjust ruler. Our easiest escape is to blame the West for all the ills of the East. We have to search our own souls and ask ourselves where in this holy book does it say that we have to be addressed every Friday by bigots, hypocrites, liars and give unholy allegiance to the despotic rulers we have today in the Muslim kingdoms? Where does it say that women can't drive? Forget leading prayers, most women can't even enter a mosque except by the kitchen. Where does it say to look down upon and humiliate people who don't conform to our way of thinking? We know where this comes from but as they say in Canada, we won't even go there. We'll concentrate on the fact that the *Qur'an* repeatedly reminds us that humanity is one community.

As an interfaith advocate, let me assure you that all is not doom and gloom. Each religion has its own problems to deal with and we should leave it to them to sort out, while we concentrate on ours. If we stop following the principal of *amal bil maroof—nahi anal munkir*—enjoin that which is good and condemn that which is wrong—we will always give others an excuse to usurp our lands, widow our women and orphan our children.

Today, it doesn't matter who leads prayers. This event is just to break the domination of a few misguided bigots who try to reduce

God to a policeman and whose only interest in "profit" is the kind that comes out of their bank account.

So each one of us is empowered to take with us a message of peace, justice, equality, tolerance, compassion and open mindedness. This is not my message or that of our host–this is the message of the book!

The Indispensible Leadership of Women

February 25, 2006

This was a paper presented in Paris for a conference titled "Women's Leadership Indispensable in the Fight Against Radicalization". The conference was hosted by WAFE dvg Women Against Fundamentalism and for Equality.

One of the warning signs of Fundamentalisms has been identified by WLUML (Women Living Under Muslim Laws)[2] as anti-women policies. Whether it's racism against women, opposition to speaking out, forced veiling by the Taliban; whether it's attacks on freedom of movement or their rights to education and work under dictatorial regimes, the leaders of these movements are always men, and the victims are always women.

According to Dr. Riffat Hasan, a scholar of Islam, the challenge before women in general, and Muslim women in particular, is to shift from the reactive mind-set, in which it is necessary for women to assert their autonomy over their lives in the face of strong opposition from patriarchal structures and systems of thought and behavior, to a pro-active mind-set, in which they can finally begin to speak of themselves as full and autonomous human beings who have not only a body but also a mind and a spirit.

The struggle for Gender equality combined with the struggle for leadership among Muslim women is close to my heart and soul. It's also imperative to the battle against fundamentalism.

---

[2] www.wluml.org

Two recent incidents in Canada made me very conscious of our fragile place in society and the need to move ahead in the direction of empowering Muslim women to become ACCEPTED AND ACKNOWLEDGED as leaders.

Soon after the 7/7 bombings in London, the Canadian PM decided to meet with leaders of the Canadian Muslim community. Who do you think he met? Ten imams of ten mosques. Some of them are misogynist and extremist self-appointed leaders. This was a wake-up call.

In the wake of the Danish cartoon controversy, when media wanted to speak with Muslim leaders, who do they choose? Once again, two conservative Imams–they didn't even ASK or bother to find out if there is leadership among Muslim women–it's taken for granted that the only leaders are men.

It seems that mainstream western media can't seem to move beyond the stereotypical image of Muslim women as meek, non-contributing members of society. As a result the achievements and leadership efforts of many Muslim women are buried under an avalanche of mis-information. It's impossible to have a conversation about Muslim women without invoking the four letter word–the veil.

So you can see what challenges we face! However, not one to back off I continue the Jihad–the struggle to be prove that education, empowerment and emancipation are essential to our lives today.

It's been said that the road to authority is tough for women– once they get there it's a bed of thorns. I have chosen to lie in this bed because unless we feel the pain, there will be no gain.

I grew up in a culture where women were supposed to be seen and not heard. So I personally call the move to RE-CLAIM my rights as a Muslim woman–the silent revolution and I can tell you that it takes up my entire life.

When I wanted to know who my leadership role models are, I went back into the history of Islam . Not the one that has been written and interpreted by male scholars who for 1400 years have told us about our rights–or rather the lack of them! I did the un-thinkable–I read and interpreted the Qur'an into my life for myself

It was through the Qur'an and the works of some contemporary women leaders like Dr. Amina Wadud, Asma Barlas, Laila Maryati, Azizah al Hibri and a few good men like Dr. Khaled abou el Fadl (a self-proclaimed feminist) that I find myself blessed to be a Muslim woman today.

Let me briefly share some of that information.

The first woman of Islam was a leader in more ways than one. Khadija, the Prophet's wife was a successful businesswoman and he worked for her. She was older than him and sent him proposal for marriage. It is said that had it not been for her wealth, the fledgling Muslim community of that time would have starved and not survived. I look upon Khadija as a born leader.

It was with her counsel and support, that the Prophet and Islam gave rights to women, saving them from being buried alive at birth, giving them rights to work, inheritance and a choice in marriage and divorce when it is only in the early 1900's that Canadian women were declared persons and only in the last century that British women were allowed to keep their earned wages.

The Prophet and Khadija's grand-daughter Zainab became a leader because she had no choice. When the men of her family were slaughtered, she took over leadership and became one of the most powerful orators of her time. Do we ever hear or read about these female leaders–no of course not.

This was also a time when the mosque was an open place with men and women using it for political, social and educational purpose. Today, the only spot that women are given in a mosque is near the kitchen or basement so that they can make tea!

In the Qur'an there is mention of Queen of Sheba who was a powerful leader. A considerable number of women of the ninth and tenth centuries are mentioned in the Arabic and Persian sources for their extraordinary achievements in being poets, calligraphers or jurists. Not to forget the first mystic of Islam–Rabia al Basri. These are our intellectual leaders.

In political life, there have been no less than 40 female heads of state. 15 of them were formal sultanas or queens who had the khutba (Friday sermon) pronounced in their names and whose insignia was minted on coins.

What happened to the rights given to Muslim women and their ability to be leaders? Respect for women and their abilities as thinkers and intellectuals went downhill from the end of the 7 and 8 century.

Many reasons are attributed to this–colonization being one them.

Self appointed Caretakers of Muslim traditionalism felt threatened by the phenomenon that a significant number of women were seen in public space, that is, a space normally thought of as for men only. They see emancipated Muslim women as symbols of Westernization that is linked not only with the colonization of Muslim people by Western powers in the not-too-distant past, but also by the continuing onslaught on what they perceive to be "the integrity of the Islamic way of life" by Westerners and Westernized Muslims who uphold the West as a model for intellectual and social transformation.

Essentially religion became the reason for oppression and victimization of women

Today when a Muslim woman speaks out or is qualified to take a leadership role, she is called militant. If she speaks in ways expected of women, she is seen as an inadequate leader. If she speaks in ways expected of leaders, she is seen as an inadequate woman. Or, the favorite slur of Muslim males, too much of a feminist.

On that note let me share an amusing personal incident. Last year a reporter from a leading magazine called me and wanted to know if Islam and feminism were compatible. The first thing I explained to her is MY definition of feminism and I want to share this with you. I said that if she looks upon feminism as an external phenomenon i.e. burning your bra or baring your chest to be equal to men, then I can't relate to it and certainly would not want to be part of such a movement. If however, the feminist challenge means finding freedom of the mind and liberation of the soul, then I would say, yes Islam is in perfect sync with feminism and I am a feminist.

The resulting article was titled, "That Militant Muslim Woman". To me, leadership is manifested in different ways depending on many factors which influence our lives. In the present time, the critical element Muslim women need is freedom to educate themselves. Given the opportunity, Muslim women, like women everywhere, will become educated, pursue careers, strive to do what is best for their families and contribute positively according to their abilities. It should be obvious that the critical element Muslim women need is freedom, especially the freedom to make choices that enable them to be independent agents of positive change.

Having said the above, it's important to mention that constant exploitation of women in Islamic societies is not religious, but cultural. It stems from the huge chasm between the faith, and our knowledge of the faith–between theory and practice. Abdolkarim Soroush, an Iranian scholar has explained this phenomenon in his book, Reason, Freedom and Democracy in Islam in which he explains both why the knowledge is anti-women and why most Muslims are opposed to the idea of rethinking the ideology. He's been heavily criticized for suggesting a reform in religious knowledge and re-interpretation of the Quranic principles of the ontic equality of men and women. This criticism comes largely from the male elite because it means giving up the systems of male privilege and tell me, how many men, Muslim or non-Muslim would be open to that?

Let me also share some mind-boggling statistics. According to UNDP human development figures, there are 37 million people who have been forced from their homes; of these approximately 28 million are Muslims and of these 28 million, 22 million are women and children. Majority of Muslims live in countries where poverty is at its highest. The Muslim women of these countries have their hands full trying to dodge bullets, finding one square meal, clean drinking water, or a roof over their heads. Their lives are not 9 to 5 corporate lives–many of them have never seen a doctor, and most of them live on the edge of despair.

The UNDP specialist also asked, "Why is it that there is such a huge illiteracy rate among women in the Arab world?" Their conclusion was because of a deficit of freedom, a deficit of women's empowerment and a deficit of modern education.

Yet, despite these challenges, they are leaders in their own domain and in their own rights.

I was invited to lead mixed gender prayers in Canada last year as a sign for young Muslim women to feel empowered and find equal space in the mosque to express their spirituality. I talk about the experience in my book to prove that spiritual equality is a domain for all humans to excel in and does not have barriers of gender but, at that time, all hell broke loose. Today it's far more acceptable with some scholars saying that its not forbidden for women to lead prayers and women are taking the lead for spiritual equality.

Not to leave you with only the down side, there are major changes taking place in the lives of Muslim women the world over. I attended a leadership conference in Barcelona where I met many of these amazing women.

For some of these women, the work is being done from within the faith.

- **Sisters-in-Islam** in Malaysia are working hard to re-define sharia laws.

- Women in Morocco brought about landmark changes to the divorce law and also succeeded in having polygamy banned.

- Baobab in Africa works on empowering women to know their rights and give them leadership training.

- In Washington, Karamah provides leadership to Muslim women in teaching them Islamic jurisprudence and their own rights.

- Women's Learning Partnership holds leadership forums and one of their recommendations is to have more representation of Muslim women in International politics.

The current dilemma of Muslim women is best exemplified through the words of Ali Shariati, a scholar and outspoken proponent of women's rights:

Women who endure their traditional mould have no problem, and women who accept their new, imported mould have the problem solved for them. In between these two types of "moulded" women, there are those who can neither tolerate the inherited mould nor can surrender to the imposed new one: what should they do? These women want to choose for themselves, want to make themselves; they need a model; an ideal type. For them the question is how to become.

Let's Pull the Veil Off Our Minds

October 8, 2006

Britain's Cabinet Minister Jack Straw took a risk with his political future (his riding is predominantly Muslim) by his suggestion that Muslim women should consider removing the veil from their face.

Instead of a knee jerk reaction, Muslims should accept Mr. Straw's comments at face value, take our heads out of the sand and pull the veils off our minds. His intention was to invoke a debate, not start fireworks!

This dialogue is long overdue and it comes at a critical time for Muslims in the West. Unfortunately some ignorant and bigoted people have misused this situation to vent their angst at Muslims (e.g. the person who pulled the veil off a woman's face in England) and others will use it as a political tool and this has to be addressed.

For better understanding of the issues at stake, let me start the discussion.

Contrary to some peoples view, covering the face is not a religious requirement for Muslim women. The injunction in the Qur'an is for modesty (for both men and women). Some Muslim women interpret this as covering their head with a scarf or chador which is universally accepted.

My understanding of this stems from the fact that Islam is a religion of balance and reason. Our face is our identity and common sense requires for it to be uncovered. Furthermore, Muslim women are not supposed to cover their face when they go for *haj* (pilgrimage) or when they perform the obligatory prayer.

Of the 1.2 billion Muslims in the world spread over the globe from Malaysia to Mozambique, approximately half are women who are extremely diverse in their mode of dress. A very small percentage chooses to cover their face. In parts of the Middle East and the subcontinent, a face covering or *niqab*, is prevalent as a cultural or tribal norm. Some women have exported this practice to the Western world.

If this is cultural, then there is dire need for discussion about adapting to new cultures. Cultures evolve and change with time and place. When non Muslims travel to Saudi Arabia for example, they're not allowed to expose skin by wearing shorts or skirts. *The Committee for the Propagation of Virtue and the Prevention of Vice* (CPVPV) would arrest them. Many Westerners work and reside in Saudi, so they adapt to the new culture to make life easier for themselves.

> Muslim women have a lot to show for the strides they've made in the modern world. They were given freedom and rights 1400 years ago. Today Muslim women are traveling into space and winning Nobel Peace Prizes.

Similarly, when we come to West by choice, we adapt to many changing factors without compromising our religious beliefs. In Canada the Charter gives us religious freedom to practice our faith in any way we choose. However, we need to let go of excess cultural baggage.

Mr. Straw suggested that a covered face makes communication difficult. He's right. I just saw a video interview of a woman in England on this issue, and her voice was muffled from behind the veil. Furthermore, in Canada there is current discussion in the judicial system about the safety risk of a woman who wants to drive in a burka because peripheral vision becomes impaired. A covered face is also an identity issue while traveling.

Of course it's a given that women in the West have the right to wear as little or as much as they want. But let's talk about the larger issue.

It's a common perception that people who wear masks have something to hide. Muslim women on the other hand, have a lot to show for the strides they've made in the modern world. They were given freedom and rights 1400 years ago. Today Muslim women are traveling into space and winning Nobel peace prizes. So why the need to hide?

Perhaps this is symptomatic of a larger issue. For the sake of future generations in the West, we must understand that we are at risk of ghettoizing ourselves and being labeled "the other" if we don't get with the plan and work towards being the mainstream. If we insist that we can't change, then we're entirely to blame when we remain on the fringes of society.

Islam encourages us to progress with time, to reason and adapt to current situations without compromising our faith. By showing our face, the faith is not compromised.

This is my perspective. Let's begin the debate.

PART 5

HONOR DIARIES

In the Muslim World, Silence Falls

Originally published in National Post
August 13, 2014

In Saturday's National Post, Rex Murphy asks why there's so much outrage over Israel's response to Hamas rocket fire, but the same activists are silent about atrocities committed in Iraq, Syria and elsewhere. In the same edition, letter-writer Al Lando argues that the people who are "attacking Jewish citizens, firebombing synagogues and launching protests against all things Jewish, in the name solidarity with Palestinian victims" seem to have no objection to the "200,000 innocent non-combatants [who] are in danger of genocide" at the hands of ISIS.

Even other terrorists shun ISIS, the Islamic State of Iraq and the Levant. The brutal, merciless Sunni terrorist group has been rampaging through town after town along the Tigris and Euphrates rivers. Now they are besieging the "infidels" known as the Yazidi, a Kurdish ethnic subgroup with an obscure religion all their own. About 40,000 Yazidi have fled their homes and now are encamped on Mount Sinjur without either food or water. Within the Muslim Middle East, the Yazidi are a tiny people, easily extinguished. Western activists throw around the word "genocide" all too lightly. But atop that mountain, the word might become grimly appropriate.

> Western activists throw around the word "genocide" all too lightly. But atop that mountain, the word might become grimly appropriate.

And yet, the advance of ISIS and its horrors has inspired no campaigns of outrage in the streets of the West. No marches in Toronto or Paris. "Proportionality," a piece of international legal jargon thrown around promiscuously as a shorthand to indict Israel for its (allegedly) excessive reprisals against Hamas' (allegedly) insignificant provocations, apparently does not govern the scale of protestors' response to the world's many injustices.

Indeed, today's global events seem surreal and fictional in their evilness. The Yazidis of Iraq are facing genocide. Boko Haram and the Taliban continue their reign of terror: Horrifying, brutal, cruel and inhuman terror from beheadings to rape. Where is the outrage in the Muslim world over these atrocities?

I ask this as a Muslim activist who's exhausted, not from defending my faith, but from asking the same question over and over again for the past two decades. When I asked this question in the aftermath of 9/11, I was criticized for being a "fear-monger." Following the 7/7 terrorist attacks in the U.K., I called on the larger Muslim community to "wake up and smell the coffee before it's too late." For this, I was labelled a traitor. Later — as I uncovered and exposed the subversive agendas of Hamas, the Muslim Brotherhood, Al-Qaeda and Hezbollah—I was labelled a heretic.

Today, ISIS is indiscriminately killing women and children in Iraq. These terrorists want women to undergo female genital mutilation and cover their faces—essentially they want to push them back into the dark ages. At the same time, Yazidi women in Iraq are being kept as slaves, while their men are killed. In Pakistan, my country of birth, minorities are being persecuted with no accountability and the movement to eradicate them has been given a religious justification, so the perpetrators are celebrated as champions.

Yet, much of the so-called "civilized world" is frozen by either political correctness or ignorance. U.S. President Barack Obama would rather play golf than address the crisis unfolding all over the Muslim world. Liberal leader Justin Trudeau apparently sees no problem visiting a Wahhabi mosque with strong links to terrorism. And protesters at the Ontario legislature continue to focus their rage on Israel, rather than addressing the heinous crimes committed by Muslims.

So it falls upon the communities where these atrocities are happening to take action. And rightly so.

The world is once again asking, "where are the moderate Muslim voices to counter the evil of ISIS and other terrorist organizations?"

Let me respond by saying that I'm completely revolted by what's happening in Iraq, Syria and the rest of the Arab world. I wish I could say the same for my larger community. When a recent documentary exposed the crimes perpetrated against women in many Muslim countries was released, so-called "moderate and progressive" Muslim women opposed the cause.

I ask all Canadians to please stop asking where the moderate Muslims are. Our voices have been subsumed by the din of the mercenaries vying for power and hegemony in the Muslim world; we have become pawns in the games played by Saudi Arabia and Iran; we are shouted down by those who would lobby for political causes over human rights; and, most importantly, our communities still bask in the belief that all is well.

Statement to the
UN Human Rights Cousel

June 17, 2014

Center for Inquiry[3] (CFI) Statement at the United Nations Human Rights Council: 26th Session (June 10–27, 2014), Interactive Dialogue with WG on Discrimination against Women—Speaker: CFI Representative, Raheel Raza— Freedom of Religion and Discrimination against Women

We thank the working group for its report, and the work it has done in highlighting the various and numerous manifestations of discrimination against women.

We note that the report observes that some states maintain discriminatory legislation, "including through the delegation of authority to religious personal law systems, obstructing women's participation in the labour market" .

While we wholeheartedly agree with this observation, we would extend the ramifications of religious personal law systems to instituting a much wider system of discrimination. Equality for women and girls is consistently and glaringly being undermined in the name of religion. We see it globally; in Saudi Arabia for example, where a religious medieval male guardianship system limits the movement of women , and where state support continues for religious groups who reinforce obscurantist views that undermine the participation of women in public life . Or in areas of Pakistan, where religious extremists are threatening girls and women, preventing their right to education from being fulfilled .

There are many discriminatory practices committed against women, all defended in the name of religion and/or culture; for example, forced marriage, female genital mutilation, son preference, Islamic law, and more generally, honor-based discrimination.

---

[3] Center for Inquiry—www.centerforinquiry.net
P.O. Box 741 • Amherst, New York 14226-0741

CEDAW says that every girl and woman has the right to own her life with dignity as a human being, to be equal to men and to participate in economic, social, cultural, civil and political action . The right to manifest one's religion or belief is a central and fundamental right. However, like most rights, it is not unlimited; it cannot be abused to excuse discriminatory activities that undermine other fundamental rights, such as the right of women to be treated equally under law, their right to autonomy, health and education.

We urge the Council to do more to investigate and highlight instances where the right to freely manifest one's religion or belief is being fallaciously manipulated so as to discriminate against women and girls, control their bodies, and restrict their right to live their life as they choose.

We call on all states to better observe their obligations under CEDAW in the face of discriminatory frameworks often forced on people by state actors intent on promoting an archaic and artificially homogenous version of religious doctrine and tradition.

Finding Spiritual Friendship

Originally published in The Interfaith Pbserver
November 15, 2012

What a joy, to travel the way of the heart. ~ Rumi

The invitation came from the Centre for Christian Studies to be a presenter at their 130th Anniversary celebrations in Winnipeg. The evening's theme was Diversity, Transformation, and Hope. I was to substitute for Joy Kogawa, a fine poet who could not make it. How could I fill her shoes!? When I heard the theme, though, I said yes.

The invitation was to be in dialogue with Stan McKay, a Native elder originally from Fisher River First Nation Reserve in northern Manitoba. As a child he attended Fisher River Indian Day School and the Birtle Indian Residential School. Stan's adult life has been focused on teaching and spiritual guidance as a source of healing for individuals and for communities. He is known widely as a wise

teacher and elder, striving to educate Canadians about the consequences of colonialism in Canada, especially the policy of assimila-
tion and residential schools, and to bring healing to the deep harm
caused to Indigenous and non-Indigenous Canadians alike.

I left home, as ever, asking for signs. It was a beautiful, bright
autumn day with a blue sky and cumulous clouds. Arriving at the
hotel in Winnipeg, I was dumbstruck to see its telephone number—
1-204-786-7011. For Muslims, 786 is a numerical code for Bismillah,
an Arabic word which means "I begin in the name of God," a word
with which we begin every prayer. In the hotel room the stationary
was embossed with the word hope. Any trepidation I had about a
new place, new people, or speaking without notes was allayed. I felt
rejuvenated, anxious and hopeful all at once.

Reaching the hall, I was amazed at how many people I knew
from my years of interfaith work across Canada. We hugged like old
friends. Stan and I met privately in a room to connect. And connect
we did. As tradition deems, I took Stan a gift of tobacco, giving it to
him privately; he was so thrilled at the gesture that he told the audience. They were primarily women, mostly Christian, with a smatter-
ing of Native youth, and, I discovered later, some Muslims.

Stan McKay and Raheel Raza took Rumi as my muse, and Stan
brought a book of readings titled God is Red. I also took a CD of
Sufi chanting which was played as people came into the hall. We were
supposed to be in a facilitated dialogue. But as we sat facing each
other and started talking, the 250+ audience faded away, and it
seemed we were two souls speaking as one. Stan and I clicked heart-
to-heart and shared ruminations, readings, and a new friendship.

Stan shared a story about dreams. Since first arriving in Canada,
I have been fascinated with the Native ethos. In many ways it corre-
sponds with the spiritual message of my own faith, so often
drowned in the din of dogma. Native communities are very diverse,
Stan observed, and while interfaith dialogue thrives, intrafaith conversation (where you talk to different communities within your own
tradition) is sadly neglected. I had to tell him the same is true in our
Muslim communities.

He asked me about diversity within the Islamic faith. He and the audience were both surprised as I explained the different denominations and sects within Islam they had never heard about. We agreed that unity does not mean uniformity and that diversity is a divine blessing. However we also agreed that people can't be forced to 'like' each other and move into a group hug until our differences are recognized and respected.

I shared the following reading on diversity from Rumi:

Every war and every conflict between human beings has happened because of some disagreement about names.
It is such an unnecessary foolishness,
because just beyond the arguing
there is a long table of companionship
set and waiting for us to sit down.
What is praised is one, so the praise is one too,
many jugs being poured into a huge basin.
All religions, all this singing, one song.
The differences are just illusion and vanity.
Sunlight looks a little different on this wall
than it does on that wall
and a lot different on this other one,
but it is still one light.
We have borrowed these clothes,
these time-and-space personalities,
from a light, and when we praise,
we are pouring them back in.

We shared our thoughts about transformation. Stan spoke of the painful experiences of colonization and the residential schools. The wounds have been deep, leaving anger and conflict in Native communities, especially among young people who have no way to channel their anger. He spoke about his own transition from anger to hope and peace. The key is recognizing that a wrong has been done in history; creating awareness of it; and then working towards forgiveness. The official movement for this in Canada is the Truth and Reconciliation Commission, on which I've served.

Jalal ad-Dīn Rumi

Stan told a wonderful story about a grandfather. He told his grandson, "Each of us has two wolves in our heart. One is a good, protective wolf. The other is a mean and violent wolf. The grandson asked, "Which wolf is stronger?" The grandfather replied, "The one you feed the most." Wow. I am trying to share just such stories with my own grandsons, an old forgotten habit. They listen in fascination.

I shared how my life has been a journey of change and transformation. I am not the person I was 25 years ago, and much of my journey towards spirituality has been in Canada, where I find myself free to pursue the different paths that lead to the same Creator. Change is positive, Stan and I agreed. And since the world is changing so fast, if we want to be part of the larger change, we need to transform ourselves as well, welcoming both difficulties and blessings. Rumi says "If you are irritated by every rub, how will your mirror be polished?"

We spoke of hope and I shared that I'm an eternal optimist. For me the glass is always half full. Stan works in healing circles and shared his hopes. The concept of circle brought us all together. The logo of our host, the Centre of Christian Studies, is a circle. Aboriginal people are very circle oriented, and Sufis embrace the circle as the circle of life. Our connections grew stronger as we talked. Both of us were able to share the difficulties of our spiritual journeys and the riches we encounter on the way. We were honoured to be able to showcase the spiritual messages from our different traditions.

After an hour, we stopped for questions, and the conversation continued. We could have talked all night!

Reconfirming the Message of *Honor Diaries* to the U.N.

Originally reported on the Honor Diaries Blog
July 4, 2014

I have been coming to the United Nations Human Rights Council for five years and lamented at the lack of women' s issues being in the forefront. The documentary *Honor Diaries* which was released in March 2014 highlighted some of the atrocities committed against women worldwide and this film created (in my opinion) the first round of awareness that practices like FGM are spreading like an epidemic and need to be discussed openly. *Honor Diaries* is the film that breaks the barriers of silence and says that "Culture is no excuse for abuse".

It came as a pleasant surprise therefore to arrive at the UN and find that on Monday June 16, a special High-level panel discussion had been convened for the entire morning regarding "The Identification of good practices in combating FGM".

In her opening remarks, Ms. Navi Pillay, UN High Commissioner for Human Rights confirmed the *Honor Diaries* statistics that more than 125 million girls and women have been subjected to FGM. Ms. Pillay said "FGM... generates profoundly damaging irreversible and life-long physical damage... FGM represents a way to exercise control over women".

Its not a co-incidence that these are the very terms used in *Honor Diaries* when speaking of FGM and trying to explain this horrific practice of genital cutting to western audiences.

Another point made by one the of the panelists, Ms. Nakpa Polo, Ambassador and Permanent Representative of Togo was "Human Rights are part of our culture and our culture does not include FGM".

Ms. Marleen Temmerman, Director Department of Reproductive Health Research, World Health Organization spoke about the need to work with schools, media and Parliamentarians to create awareness—something that *Honor Diaries* is already doing.

Ms. Pillay also spoke about child marriage which was discussed at a later session.

Honoring Girls

Originally posted on Raheel's blog
July 28, 2014

It was a great honour to be invited to attend The Girl Summit[4] in UK which was hosted by the UK Government and United Nations Children's Fund.

But before I got there, I had to get a badge. Having experienced government bureaucracy in other countries, it was a pleasant surprise to reach Whitehall and find everything in order. That's when I first discovered that there are 600 delegates coming to the Summit. We were told that the program will only be available at the entrance.

So I made my way to Walworth Academy on 22 July early in the morning. The security was very tight and media swarmed all over the place. When I got the program I understood why. Starting with Ban Ki-Moon in the opening plenary to Sheikh Hasina Prime Minister of Bangladesh and David Cameron, it was a high profile event.

The theme of the Summit was "A Future Free from FGM and Child and Force Marriage". As an activist for women's rights my entire adult life, I know how hard it has been to bring women's issues on the front burner. Especially those issues that are taboo to discuss or debate. So it was with great pleasure that I started listening to the conversation around me.

When the documentary *Honor Diaries* was released, one of the criticisms against it was "why is the focus on Muslim Majority Societies?" Well I got the answer at the Summit. Today in areas of the Muslim world ruled by despots like ISIS and Boko Haram, forced and underage marriage and FGM are being promoted—while in UK

---

[4] www.girlsummitpledge.com

a country where these practices did not originate, an International charter is being drawn up to end FGM and forced/child marriages in this generation. I felt proud and motivated to be part of the *Honor Diaries* movement which is still cutting-edge in breaking the barriers of silence.

Speaking of *Honor Diaries*, I was inspired by the number of women at the Summit who had seen the film and commented on it. Jaha Dukuray found me in the crowd although she was being filmed by The Guardian, and we had a few moments of bonding.

All VIP's were welcomed into the summit compound by the "Pandemonium Drummers" so when we heard drumming, we knew someone important was entering. This is how I saw Malala Yousafzai and her father walk in. I ran up to Malala to give her an *Honor Diaries* scarf and her handlers tried to brush me off but I said "Malala belongs to the same heritage as I am from, so her movement belongs to all of us and I am from her homeland". I managed to gift her a DVD and scarf before she was whisked away.

Later I went to the Plenary and on the way I saw the VIP and media room so I just walked in with my journalist cap on. Here I was able to meet many people face-to-face. An African girl walked upto me and said "you are my hero". I was a bit taken aback. She introduced herself as Alimatu Dimoneken who is an FGM survivor and had seen *Honor Diaries*. She said my family reminded her of her family. I also met Malala's father and gave him another DVD just to ensure that he has a copy. He promised to visit when he comes to Canada as we spoke the same language. Then I met John Baird, Minister of Foreign Affairs for Canada. As a fellow-Canadian I was proud of his being the facilitator for a session on Action for Change. I also met Gordon Campbell, our Canadian High Commissioner in Britain. All of them spoke out against FGM and Forced/Child Marriage. Hina Jilani, Supreme Court Advocate from Pakistan was there and she said "It's time to make Governments accountable for their duties towards their citizens and International relations need to be strengthened to change social policy."

At a later session Malala was on a panel with Sheikh Hasina. Malala spoke about her visit to Nigeria to meet with the families of the girls kidnapped by Boko Haram. She is an impressive and eloquent speaker (without notes) and she said "It's we who create a culture in which women can't be educated—so we can change those cultures that go against human rights". Her solution—educate all girls. Sheikh Hasina spoke about a move in Bangladesh to make education free for all girls until graduation.

Heads of African States spoke about commitments, targets and change. But nowhere is the change more obvious than in the UK where the problems have been immense but so too have the solutions.

Prime Minister David Cameron made a surprise appearance. He spoke with great conviction about the changes made in the UK legal, Justice and Educational systems to tackle FGM and Child/Forced Marriage. Not only have they invested finances into this movement, but man power and well. He said it's now mandatory in UK for teachers and doctors to report signs of FGM or forced/child marriages. Parents will be convicted. At the time he spoke, 21 countries had signed up with the Girl charter as well as 230 organizations. I was able to present him with an *Honor Diaries* DVD as well.

Jasvinder Sanghera of Karma Nirvana who has appeared in *Honor Diaries* was up front and Centre having worked on forced marriages since her organization was formed. She introduced me to many of the movers and shakers in the field.

Over lunch, we had a short screening of the forced marriage clip from Honor Diaires and there were some good questions. One young South Asian girl asked "what about the victims?" and later she came to me and told me her story. She is of Pakistani origin, born and brought up in London. She was only 12 when she came home from school one day and was asked to wear a bridal dress and married off against her will to a man much older than her because the family had decided this is her future. She was not allowed to study and two years later, she gave birth to two kids. She was sent to Pakistan, came back and decided to leave her abusive husband for which she was ex-communicated from her family. She managed to educate herself and now has grown up children and spends her time counselling women like herself. The need for support systems for women in her situation became very apparent.

Later in the Summit there were celebrities like actor Freida Pinto. I left inspired by what I had experienced. If North America could only take a lesson from UK, we will have solved a huge problem that exists on this Continent as well.

A Woman's Voice at the Mosque

Originally published on the Gatestone Institute [5]
May 23, 2013

In the aftermath of the Boston bombings, Toronto and Montreal saw arrests of two Muslims charged with terror related activities. There's been some hand-wringing and questions about "what leads Muslim youth towards violence?"

Amid an array of reasoning, one constant factor that has emerged is the possible influence of Wahhabi mosques. This is not new. For years after 9/11, we were concerned about possible seditious messages coming from the pulpit, some of which I have heard.

While the sermon every Friday in the mosque may not ask Muslims outright to commit violent acts, I believe that what is not being said is the issue here.

Keeping in mind that one day soon we will be hearing women's voices in the mosque giving a sermon, if not every Friday, then, we hope, at least once a month, I decided to be prepared and have written up a sample sermon. Of course, sermons should evolve with time but this is something along the lines I would have liked my kids to have heard as they were growing up in Canada. At present Muslim women can lead prayer and offer sermons only to a congregation exclusively made up of women.

---

[5] Raheel Raza, "A Woman's Voice at the Mosque."

I begin in the name of God, the Compassionate, the Merciful. Salaam Alaikum. Peace upon all those who gather here.

Let us speak to the concept of compassion and mercy. If we want to ask God for compassion and mercy, then we must try and show the same compassion and mercy for all God's creation, which includes people of all faiths, the environment and animals.

We greet each other with the universal Muslim greeting of peace. Just saying 'peace be upon you' does not create peace. Peace is something we have to actively work towards and put into practice, because only when are at peace with ourselves, can we can spread peace towards others. Peace is also about justice so when we want justice for ourselves, we must be prepared to offer the same justice to others.

We live in a society where we meet people of diverse faiths, ethnicities and nationalities. This is a blessing and we have to learn to interact with respect and dignity. Remember when we offer our prayers five times a day, we send blessings upon the progeny of Abraham who are Jews and Christians. Today Christians are being persecuted in Muslim lands and anti-Semitism is on the rise. We must speak out when we see this happening.

Most of you are either born in the West or have chosen to live in the West. A wise man once said that your home is not the country you were born in, but the country you will die in. So whether you were born in Multan, Mangalore or Malaysia, when you become a citizen of a country in the West and death overtakes you in Sydney or London or Montreal, wherever you come from you will die as a citizen of that place.

Therefore my brothers and sisters that place is home—that is the country we have to build, fight for, live for and bring about the change we want from within.

There is a tradition in Islam where we are commanded to follow the laws of the land in which we live. Thus it is incumbent on us to obey the laws of those lands, which give us our livelihood, a roof over our heads and our bread and butter.

This does not mean that you have to accept everything you see around you. In a liberal democracy there is the beauty of disagreeing, and all of you have the right to disagree with your political leaders but there are ways of making this work. We have systems at our disposal through which we can address our discontent.

There is a profound verse in the Quran, 5:32: "As we (Allah) prescribed to the House of Israel, to kill one person, unless it is for murder or sedition, is to kill all of humanity, and to save one person is to save all of humanity." If we can keep this uppermost in our hearts and minds while teaching this to our children, we will be better human beings.

Most of all we must learn to use reason and logic and broaden the use of ijtehad–individual reasoning in religious affairs. As Qur'an mandates in verse 2:44, "Do you bid other people to be pious, while you forget your own selves–and yet you recite the divine writ? Will you not, then, use your reason?"

The next sermon will be about women's right based on the Qur'an: the account of the life of Muhammad we have received as Muslim believers, and the example of his first wife, Khadijah, who chose him for marriage. For this we hope to see women as equal participants in the mosque.

Let us pray that God grants us the wisdom and knowledge to be good human beings, exceptional citizens, and doers of good deeds.

Ameen.

AFTERWORD

by BARBARA KAY

If, even ten years ago, you had told me–the proverbial "nice Jewish girl" from Toronto, who had never had a meaningful encounter with a Muslim in her life until well into adulthood–that one day I would be writing a preface in praise of a "Muslim feminist," I would have laughed very heartily in your face.

Life is unpredictable. And so here I am ...

I first met Raheel Raza in Montreal some years ago, when she took part in a panel on Islamism. I was struck by her candor in acknowledging negative trends in Islamic societies. And charmed by her cheeky defiance of those fundamentalists who would prefer she hide her woman's body and voice under a metaphorical burka.

Since then, I've had the pleasure of getting to know Raheel better, mainly through participation in panel discussions on problematic subjects that are close to both our hearts as journalists: religious extremism, western feminism's abandonment of women in misogynistic societies and the distressing escalation of honour killings in certain cultural communities. I'm a great fan of Raheel's activism for a reformed, democratic Islam, which she tirelessly promotes through her writing, media appearances and filmmaking. I'm also a fan of Raheel personally; she is a singularly warm, personable and gracious lady with a gift for meaningful human connection.

This revised collection of essays (with new material added) chronicling Raheel's intellectual and spiritual evolution offers important insights to those readers for whom a triumphalist brand of Islam is (understandably, alas) today's norm, and who automatically associate "Muslim woman" with "veil." Raheel reminds us that while we unfortunately today often find ourselves "back in the dark ages of Islam," Islam was not always dominated by Wahhabist intransigence. There were eras when disputed interpretations of Islamic texts, some of them emphasizing the tenet of "no compulsion in religion," were well tolerated and courteously debated within Muslim society, and when Muslim women enjoyed the "liberation of the mind and soul" Raheel identifies as the core of Muslim feminism.

I particularly admire Raheel's objectivity regarding the corrosive alignment of fundamentalist Islam with longstanding South Asian and Arabic patriarchism. Her forthrightness in treating the scourge of honour-based violence against girls and women–including her brave refusal to grasp the tempting rhetorical lifeline of "domestic violence" to explain it–does her singular credit. Indeed, I was pleased to write a column last March in the National Post extolling her recent film, *Honor Diaries*, which makes that point painfully clear.

"We have been alienated from our religious tradition," Raheel writes. She aspires to expose "the schizophrenia that has seeped into Islam," advocating reform that emphasizes women's rights. Denounced as a "traitor," a "heretic" and a "fear-monger" for demanding change, Raheel nevertheless soldiers on. Drawing encouragement from the supportive men in her life–loving husband and sons, now two grandsons as well–and inspiration from both Islam's very first women of influence as well as from modern Muslim scholars, Raheel proposes a rights movement that does not ask for invented new rights, but that proposes to "reclaim my rights as a Muslim woman."

I wish Raheel well on her often arduous and sometimes lonely journey. It is not often that two such "daughters of Abraham" find common cause in this tumultuous and riven world, and the collegial time that I share with Raheel is for that reason all the more cherished. I hope this eloquent and hopeful book will find its way to women everywhere, especially to those who are denied Raheel's voice, but do share Raheel's yearning for change.

When a fellow congregant has finished reading a short portion of the Torah during Shabbat services, we Jews say to him or her, "ya'asher ko'ach," which means "may your strength remain firm." Ya'asher ko'ach to you, Raheel. May this book, in which we are all stakeholders, take your uplifting mission, with God's blessing, from strength to strength in Muslim communities everywhere.

Barbara Kay

Bibliography

Bakhtiar, Laleh. *Shariati on Shariati and the Muslim Woman*. Kazi Publications, 1996.

Chittick, William C. *The Sufi Path of Love: The Spiritual Teachings of Rumi*. State University of New York Press, 1983.

Feiler, Bruce. *Abraham: A Journey to the Heart of Three Faiths*. Harper Perennial, 2005.

Hassan, Riffat. *Women's Rights and Islam: From the I. C. P. D. to Beijing*. Privately Printed C. 1995, 1111.

Lang, Jeffrey. *Losing My Religion: A Call For Help*. amana, 2004.

Mernissi, Fatima. *Beyond the Veil, Revised Edition: Male-Female Dynamics in Modern Muslim Society*. Revised Edition. Indiana University Press, 1987.

Mir-Hosseini, Ziba. *Islam and Gender*. Princeton University Press, 1999.

"Official Website of Raheel Raza." *Raheel Raza*. Accessed September 1, 2010. www.raheelraza.com.

Raheel Raza. "A Woman's Voice at the Mosque." *Gatestone Institute*, May 23, 2013. www.gatestoneinstitute.org/3725/mosques-women.

— — —. "Honoring Girls." *Raheel Raza's Blog*, July 28, 2014. http://raheelraza.wordpress.com/2014/07/28/387/.

— — —. "How a Native Elder & a Muslim Found Spiritual Friendship at a Christian Celebration." *The Interfaith Observer*, November 15, 2012. http://theinterfaithobserver.org/journal-articles/2012/11/15/how-a-native-elder-a-muslim-found-spiritual-friendship-at-a.html.

Raza, Raheel. "Raheel Tells UN Human Rights Council - 'Culture Is No Excuse for Abuse', Reconfirming the Message of Honor Diaries." *Honor Diaries Blog*, June 26, 2014. www.honordiaries.com/blog/raheel-tells-un-human-rights-council-culture-excuse-abuse/.

Sachedina, Abdulaziz. *The Islamic Roots of Democratic Pluralism*. Oxford University Press, USA, 2007.

Safi, Omid. *Progressive Muslims: On Justice, Gender, and Pluralism*. Oneworld Publications, 2003.

Schwartz, Stephen. *The Two Faces of Islam: Saudi Fundamentalism and Its Role in Terrorism*. First. Anchor, 2003.

Soroush, Abdolkarim. *Reason, Freedom, and Democracy in Islam: Essential Writings of Abdolkarim Soroush*. Oxford University Press, USA, 2002.

Tucker, Judith E. *In the House of the Law: Gender and Islamic Law in Ottoman Syria and Palestine*. 1st ed. University of California Press, 2000.

Wadud, Amina. *Qur'an and Woman: Rereading the Sacred Text from a Woman's Perspective*. Oxford University Press, USA, 1999.

About the Author

Raheel Raza is President of The Council for Muslims Facing Tomorrow, author of the book *Their Jihad... Not My Jihad*, award winning journalist, public speaker & activist for human rights featured in the award-winning documentary *Honor Diaries*.

She is recipient of the Queen Elizabeth II Diamond Jubilee medal for service to Canada.

Raheel bridges the gap between East and West, promoting cultural and religious diversity for which she has appeared globally on International media, including on CNN and FOX News.

Raheel has been invited to speak locally at places of worship, the private sector, the Justice Department, School Boards and government institutions. Internationally she has addressed audiences at Universities in USA including Harvard & Columbia, in UK at Oxford and Cambridge, other forums across Australia and Europe and the Israeli Presidential Conference in Jerusalem.

In her pursuit for human rights, Raheel is accredited with United Nations Human Rights Council in Geneva through Centre for Inquiry (CFI). She has received many awards for her work on women's equality including the City of Toronto's Constance Hamilton award and the Urban Hero award. She is the first Muslim woman in Canada to lead mixed gender prayers.

Raheel has made a documentary film called *Whose Sharia is it anyway?* dealing with the sharia debate in Ontario, Canada. She runs a Forum for Learning for youth to educate them about the dangers of radicalization and terrorism, and continues to write and speak about the subject. Raheel is Distinguished Senior Fellow with The Gatestone Institute. She also sits on the Advisory Board of The ACTV Foundation (The Alliance of Canadian Terror Victims).

www.muslimsfacingtomorrow.com

raheel@raheelraza.com

http://raheelraza.wordpress.com

Made in the USA
Middletown, DE
06 March 2016